AUTUMN & WINTER
COZY DINNER COOKBOOK

The Best Traditional Recipes for Warming Dinners, Holiday Roasts, a Thanksgiving Turkey, Christmas Baking, Bread, Warm Drinks and More

William Lawrence

© Copyright by William Lawrence 2021 - All rights reserved.

The content contained within this book may not be reproduced, duplicated or transmitted without direct written permission from the author or the publisher.

Under no circumstances will any blame or legal responsibility be held against the publisher, or author, for any damages, reparation, or monetary loss due to the information contained within this book. Either directly or indirectly. You are responsible for your own choices, actions, and results.

Legal Notice:

This book is copyright protected. This book is only for personal use. You cannot amend, distribute, sell, use, quote or paraphrase any part, or the content within this book, without the consent of the author or publisher.

Disclaimer Notice:

Please note the information contained within this document is for educational and entertainment purposes only. All effort has been executed to present accurate, up to date, and reliable, complete information. No warranties of any kind are declared or implied. Readers acknowledge that the author is not engaging in the rendering of legal, financial, medical or professional advice. The content within this book has been derived from various sources. Please consult a licensed professional before attempting any techniques outlined in this book.

By reading this document, the reader agrees that under no circumstances is the author responsible for any losses, direct or indirect, which are incurred as a result of the use of the information contained within this document, including, but not limited to, — errors, omissions, or inaccuracies.

Leave a review about our book:

As an independent author with a small marketing budget, reviews are my livelihood on this platform. If you enjoyed this book, I'd really appreciate it, if you left your honest feedback. You can do so by clicking review button.

I love hearing my readers and I personally read every single review!

Table of Contents

INTRODUCTION 8
HOLIDAY ROASTS 11
    STUFFED CHICKEN 12
    APRICOT GLAZED TURKEY 14
    HONEY GLAZED DUCK 16
    STUFFED GOOSE 18
    CRUSTED RIB ROAST 20
    BEEF TENDERLOIN 22
    SPICED LAMB SHOULDER 24
    HERBED LEG OF LAMB 26
    SPICED PORK SHOULDER 28
    HONEY GLAZED HAM 30
TURKEY RECIPES 32
    GLAZED TURKEY BREAST 33
    STUFFED TURKEY BREAST 34
    GRILLED WHOLE TURKEY 36
    TURKEY & SWEET POTATO CHILI 38
    TURKEY & VEGGIE POT PIE 40
    TURKEY CORDON BLEU CASSEROLE 42
    TURKEY & PUMPKIN PASTA 44
    TURKEY MEATLOAF 46
    TURKEY PINWHEELS 48
    TURKEY & CRANBERRY BURGERS 50
WARM POULTRY DISHES 51
    CHEESY BUFFALO CHICKEN 52
    CHICKEN ROULADE 54
    CHICKEN WITH BUTTERNUT SQUASH 56
    CHICKEN WITH PEARS 58
    CHICKEN & PUMPKIN CURRY 60
    CHICKEN IN ORANGE SAUCE 62
    CHICKEN IN FIG SAUCE 64
    STUFFED CORNISH HENS 66
    PESTO CHICKEN BAKE 68
    CHICKEN IN CRANBERRY SAUCE 69
MEAT MAINS 70
    GLAZED FILET MIGNON 71

- Beef Stroganoff 72
- Beef Wellington 74
- Shepherd's Pie 76
- Glazed Pork Ribs 78
- Cranberry & Apple Stuffed Pork Chops 80
- Sausage & Bacon Bread Casserole 82
- Braised Lamb Shanks 84
- Pan-Seared Lamb Chops 86
- Pork with Brussels Sprouts 88

FISH & SEAFOOD 89

- Stuffed Salmon 90
- Salmon Pie 92
- Scalloped Oysters 94
- Tuna Casserole 96
- Shrimp & Tomato Bake 98
- Seafood Casserole 100
- Tilapia & Tomato Casserole 102
- Creamy Salmon Casserole 103
- Seared Tuna 104
- Bacon-Wrapped Salmon 105

WARM SOUPS & STEWS 106

- Lentil & Sweet Potato Soup 107
- Turkey & Wild Rice Soup 108
- Bacon & Tortellini Soup 110
- French Onion Soup 112
- Creamy Pumpkin Soup 114
- Chicken & Mushroom Stew 116
- Turkey & Pasta Stew 118
- Beef Stew in a Pumpkin 120
- Pork Stew 122
- Potato & Bean Stew 124

VEGETARIAN & VEGAN SIDE DISHES 126

- Rosemary Mushrooms 127
- Potato Mash 128
- Roasted Tomatoes 129
- Roasted Cauliflower 130
- Glazed Carrots 132
- Nutty Brussels Sprouts 134
- Glazed Sweet Potatoes 136
- Baked Beans 138

BUTTERED RICE 140
BUTTERED QUINOA 142

SALADS 143

CITRUS SALAD 144
CHICKEN & CRANBERRY SALAD 145
CHICKEN CAESAR SALAD 146
BACON & CORN SALAD 148
CRANBERRY & SPINACH SALAD 150
BEET & WALNUT SALAD 152
FIG SALAD 154
PORK & ORANGE SALAD 156
STEAK & PEAR SALAD 157
KALE & BRUSSELS SPROUT SALAD 158

BREADS 159

DRIED FRUIT BREAD 160
PERSIMMON & DATE BREAD 162
APPLE BREAD 164
CHOCOLATY BANANA BREAD 166
CRANBERRY & ORANGE BREAD 168
CRANBERRY & PUMPKIN BREAD 170
PUMPKIN BREAD 172
CHOCOLATY PUMPKIN BREAD 174
ZUCCHINI & CARROT BREAD 176
BRAIDED LEMON BREAD 178

STARTERS 180

BACON-WRAPPED BRUSSELS SPROUTS 181
GLAZED MEATBALLS 182
BLACK BEAN MEATBALLS 184
BACON & CHEESE TRUFFLES 186
VEGGIE BALLS 188
PARMESAN SHRIMP 190
COCONUT SHRIMP 192
FRIED RAVIOLI 194
VEGGIE LATKES 196
JALAPENO POPPERS 198

SAUCES & STAPLES 200

PUMPKIN PIE SPICE 201
CRANBERRY JAM 202
CRANBERRY & APPLE RELISH 204

CRANBERRY SAUCE 206
FIG & RAISINS CHUTNEY 208
RAISIN & ORANGE CHUTNEY 210
BBQ SAUCE 212
MULLING SPICES 214
SPICE RUB 215
HONEY MUSTARD 216

BAKING (COOKIES, CAKES, PIES, TARTS) 217

GINGERBREAD COOKIES 218
DOUBLE CHOCOLATE COOKIES 220
MERINGUE COOKIES 222
APPLE CAKE 224
CHOCOLATE PUMPKIN CAKE 226
CRANBERRY UPSIDE-DOWN CAKE 228
PUMPKIN PIE 230
CHOCOLATE TART 232
MINI ALMOND TARTS 234
APPLE PIE 236

DESSERTS 238

STRAWBERRY & BANANA TRIFLE 239
NO-BAKE BANANA PUDDING 240
CRANBERRY & ORANGE MOUSSE 242
PUMPKIN CRÈME BRÛLÉE 244
CHOCOLATE CUSTARD 246
ORANGE CUPCAKES 248
PUMPKIN BROWNIES 250
CRANBERRY, APPLE & PEAR CRISP 252
BREAD & RAISINS PUDDING 254
STUFFED APPLES 256

WARM AROMATIC TEAS 258

JUNIPER BERRY TEA 259
ORANGE TEA 260
MINT GREEN TEA 261
LEMONY GINGER TEA 262
LEMONY GREEN TEA 263
GINGER & TURMERIC TEA 264
PASSION FRUIT TEA 265
SPICED MILK TEA 266
APPLE TEA 267
CRANBERRY TEA 268

HOT ALCOHOLIC COCKTAILS..270
- JAMAICA COFFEE COCKTAIL...271
- LEMONY WHISKEY 272
- SPIKED LATTE 273
- BUTTERED RUM 274
- SPIKED MATCHA 275
- MULLED CIDER 276
- MULLED WINE 277
- WINE HOT CHOCOLATE 278
- BOURBON EGGNOG..280
- CRANBERRIES & CINNAMON COCKTAIL 282

HOT NON-ALCOHOLIC COCKTAILS..283
- BUTTERED PINEAPPLE MOCKTAIL 284
- SPICED CIDER 285
- CRANBERRY CIDER 286
- HOT WASSAIL 287
- HOT CHOCOLATE 288
- ORANGE MOCHA 289
- ORANGE ATOLE 290
- CRANBERRY MOCKTAIL 291
- GINGERBREAD LATTE 292
- RASPBERRY HOT CHOCOLATE 293

CONCLUSION 294

Introduction

The cold winter days are right around the corner, and it is that time of the year when you anticipate eating homemade meals and delightful treats with your loved ones. Our need for warming and comforting food grows as the season changes. It is common that the foods you have been contentedly consuming all spring and summer suddenly become intolerable when the winter sets in. This is true if you have recently started a new diet. Continuing your summer diet is just not possible now with the emerging desire to cook warming and rich winter meals. We understand your food cravings and that is why this cookbook will provide you with delicious, intriguing, and warming meal ideas to enjoy this winter. The 160 recipes shared in this cookbook are perfect for special occasions and holidays or for routine dinners with your loved ones. If you are interested in the idea of cooking delicious food during the holidays, then also try our **Complete Holiday Cookbook** to find special recipes for all special celebrations.

Winter Foodie Alert!

As the weather cools, your body seeks food that will warm it up. Salads and watermelon, which go like hot cakes in July, are no longer as refreshing and in demand come winter. They make us feel even colder, which can lead to a desire for sugar to warm us up. Warming foods during the fall and winter season become more vital as the season moves toward its peak. Although it may still be warm enough for a salad in September, a delicious, heated stew in October is far more appealing. By the time November arrives, our bodies are craving a warm, homemade dinner consisting of winter vegetables like squash, potatoes, and carrots. Such a meal can warm you from the inside out and provide your body with natural carbohydrates that will lift your spirits on a gloomy day. You may also notice that your sugar cravings subside and that the cold weather has become more enjoyable. From the inside out, you're getting warmer.

Warming Food for fall and Winter

Whether you are making a delicious stew or cooking a warming bowl of hot soup for a cold winter evening, there must be some comforting ingredients in your food. These ingredients will not only keep you warm but will also provide the much needed nourishment to survive through the winters.

Root vegetables

Root vegetables like turnips, radishes, and sweet potatoes are loaded with starch, and their complex carb content can help you keep warm in the winter.

Thermogenesis is the process by which your body produces heat as a result of food metabolization. This means, foods that take longer to digest can assist in increasing your body temperature! Because root vegetables take longer to digest, use them in roasted dinners or hearty soups this winter to keep your body warm.

Complex carbohydrates

As it is chilly outside during winter, we may feel more hungry than usual; overeating doesn't seem to help either. Only eating sensibly can help! It is tempting to munch all day on chocolate bars, biscuits, and other snacks, but simple or refined carbohydrates break down rapidly and don't keep you warm for very long. Only eating complex carbohydrates like those found in whole grains, fruits, and veggies are going to help you.

Bananas

Bananas are a great nutritious option to add over your oatmeal or porridge in the morning! Bananas are high in vitamin B and magnesium, which support the functioning of your thyroid and adrenal glands. Our body temperature is regulated by these glands. As a result, a banana a day keeps the shivers away!

Eggs

Eggs are sometimes referred to as a "powerhouse of energy" since they not only keep your body warm but are also high in proteins and vitamins. They can also assist your body in fighting infections throughout the winter.

Coffee

Yes, here is a perfect excuse to indulge yourself in your coffee addiction! The caffeine in coffee boosts your metabolism, which can lead to a rise in body temperature, so go ahead and sip that extra cup of coffee!

Hot ginger tea

For those who aren't excited about the prospect of extra caffeine, try a cup of hot ginger tea. Ginger is a diaphoretic ingredient which means that it can induce thermogenesis, giving you double the warmth! It increases your metabolism, aids digestion, and even helps to warm your fingers and toes by increasing blood flow. If you don't like ginger tea, you can use it in soups, stews, and even smoothies, so don't skip out on this wintertime favorite!

More spices

You must include cinnamon, cumin, sesame seeds, pepper, and turmeric in your cooking, in addition to ginger. Many people believe that hot chili sauce is the way to go; however, it really cools you off by making you perspire somewhat. Cumin, on the other hand, produces a more mild heat and thus keeps you warm for longer. Turmeric is less hot than red chili, but it adds heat to dishes and can even be mixed into milk or tea.

Cinnamon also increases your metabolism, which elevates your body warmth, and it goes well with warm drinks like hot chocolate and lattes. Adding fragrant cinnamon to soup is, of course, also warming and tasty!

Finally, white and black pepper, as well as sesame seeds, are excellent for staying healthy throughout the winter. Pepper protects against the winter flu, while sesame seeds aid in the treatment of more serious respiratory disorders such as pneumonia, bronchitis, and asthma.

Iron-rich foods
You may have anemia or an iron deficiency if your hands and feet are constantly cold. Iron is necessary for transporting oxygen everywhere in the body. Red meat, spinach, black beans (which are also a fantastic protein source because they don't contain saturated fat), poultry, lentils, and iron-fortified cereals all contain a lot of iron, so they are important in winter meals.

Ghee
Ghee is not only easy to digest, but it also boosts immunity by protecting against the flu and the common cold. It also helps to strengthen bones. It's easy to incorporate ghee into your diet by simply cooking with it instead of using oil.

Dry fruits and nuts
You may also sprinkle these on top of your oatmeal or porridge, or just eat them as a snack to avoid those unhealthy chocolate bars. Almonds, cashews, and raisins are examples of dry fruits and nuts that generate heat in the body and can also aid with iron deficiency.

Water
If you become cold easily, you may need to increase your water intake. Water helps maintain the optimal body temperature, which may seem counterintuitive given that we are less thirsty in cooler temperatures. Your core temperature actually drops when you're dehydrated. Having a water bottle on hand is an excellent way to remind yourself to stay hydrated.

HOLIDAY ROASTS

There is nothing more satifying than a warming, delicious roast. Whether it is chicken, beef or duck, the wide array of seasonings and flavors will keep your soul happy.

For most of these recipes you will need a roasting pan, brush, meat thermometer, and baster.

Temperatures for meat:

* Poultry and fowl – 165°F

* Meat steaks, chops and roasts – 145°F

STUFFED CHICKEN 12
APRICOT GLAZED TURKEY 14
HONEY GLAZED DUCK 16
STUFFED GOOSE 18
CRUSTED RIB ROAST 20
BEEF TENDERLOIN 22
SPICED LAMB SHOULDER 24
HERBED LEG OF LAMB 26
SPICED PORK SHOULDER 28
HONEY GLAZED HAM 30

Stuffed Chicken

Preparation time: 15 minutes

Cooking time: 1 hour 15 minutes

Total time: 1 hour 30 minutes

Servings: 8

Ingredients:

- 2½ tablespoons unsalted butter
- 1/3 cup onion, chopped finely
- ½ cup onion, sliced
- 1/3 cup carrots, peeled and chopped finely
- ½ cup carrot, peeled and sliced
- 1/3 cup celery, chopped finely
- 2 fresh thyme sprigs
- 2 fresh savory sprigs
- 2-3 fresh parsley stems
- 3-4 celery leaves
- 1 lemon, cut into 1/8-inch-thick slices
- 1 tablespoon fresh lemon juice
- 1 (4-pound) whole chicken, giblets and neck removed
- Salt and ground black pepper, as required
- ¾ cup chicken broth

How to Prepare:

1. Preheat your oven to 425°F.
2. Arrange a wire rack in a large-sized roasting pan.
3. Melt 1 tablespoon of butter in a wok over medium heat and sauté the finely chopped onion, carrots, and celery for about 3-5 minutes.
4. Stir in the herb sprigs and remove from the heat.
5. Rub the cavity of chicken with salt and black pepper.
6. Then stuff the cavity with the cooked onion mixture, parsley stems, celery leaves, and lemon slices.
7. Rub the outside of the chicken with 1 tablespoon of butter.
8. Tie the ends of the drumsticks together and tuck the wings under the body.
9. Rub the chicken with salt and black pepper generously.
10. Arrange the chicken onto the prepared roasting pan, breast-side up.
11. Roast for 15 minutes.
12. Remove the roasting pan from oven and set the temperature to 350°F.
13. Now melt the remaining ½ tablespoon of butter and brush the chicken with it.
14. Arrange the carrot and onion slices around the chicken and pour in the chicken broth.
15. Roast for approximately 1 hour more.
16. After 45 minutes of roasting, brush the chicken with the lemon juice and then baste with pan juices before roasting for the remaining 15 minutes.
17. Check if the internal temperature of the meat is above 165°F.
18. Remove the roasting pan from oven and place the chicken onto a large serving platter for about 10-15 minutes before carving.
19. Cut the chicken into desired-sized pieces and serve.

Nutritional Values:

Calories 475, Total Fat 20.6 g, Saturated Fat 7 g, Cholesterol 211 mg, Sodium 323 mg, Total Carbs 2 g, Fiber 0.5 g, Sugar 1 g, Protein 66.3 g

Apricot Glazed Turkey

Preparation time: 20 minutes

Cooking time: 3 hours 40 minutes

Total time: 4 hours

Servings: 30

Ingredients:

- 1 cup apricot preserves
- 1 cup apricot nectar
- 1 tablespoon honey
- 2 tablespoons fresh ginger root, minced
- 3 tablespoons plus ½ teaspoon fresh sage, chopped
- 1 teaspoon fresh thyme, chopped
- 1½ teaspoon salt
- 1 teaspoon ground black pepper
- 1 (22-pound) whole turkey, giblets and neck removed
- ¾ cup butter, softened
- 2 cups low-sodium chicken broth

How to Prepare:

1. Preheat your oven to 400°F.
2. Arrange an oven rack in the lowest third portion of the oven.
3. Arrange a wire rack in a large-sized roasting pan.
4. In a saucepan, combine apricot preserves, nectar, honey, and ginger root over a high heat and bring to a boil.
5. Now, adjust the heat to medium-low and let the mixture simmer for about 15 minutes or until thickened, stirring frequently.
6. Remove the pan of glaze from the heat and set aside.
7. Meanwhile, in a bowl, blend together 3 tablespoons of sage, butter, salt, and black pepper. Set aside.
8. Rub the turkey with butter mixture generously.
9. Arrange the turkey into the prepared roasting pan, breast side up.
10. With a spatula, loosen the skin over each side of the breastbone.
11. Coat the turkey with apricot glaze underneath the loosened skin and all over the skin generously, leaving ¾ cup of glaze for later.
12. With kitchen twine, tie both legs together at the bottom.
13. Roast for approximately 30 minutes.
14. Now, set the oven to 325°F.
15. Roast for 1½ hours, coating with pan juices occasionally.
16. Now, cover the turkey with a large piece of foil and roast for approximately 45 minutes.
17. Add the broth, thyme and remaining sage in the roasting pan around the turkey and roast for approximately 15 minutes.
18. Remove the piece of foil and coat the turkey with ½ cup of apricot glaze.
19. Roast for 40 minutes, coating with glaze occasionally.
20. Check if the internal temperature of the meat is above 165°F.
21. Remove the roasting pan from oven and transfer the turkey onto a large serving platter.
22. Using a piece of foil, cover the turkey for about 15-20 minutes before carving.
23. Cut the turkey into desired-sized pieces and serve.

Nutritional Values:

Calories 640, Total Fat 21.3 g, Saturated Fat 8.4 g, Cholesterol 264 mg, Sodium 391 mg, Total Carbs 8.8 g, Fiber 0.1 g, Sugar 5.2 g, Protein 97.7 g

Honey Glazed Duck

Preparation time: 15 minutes

Cooking time: 3 hours

Total time: 3¼ hours

Servings: 12

Ingredients:

- 1 (6-pound) whole duck, giblets removed
- Salt, as required
- 1 lemon, sliced
- 5 garlic cloves, sliced
- ½ cup balsamic vinegar
- 1/3 cup honey
- 2 tablespoons fresh lemon juice

How to Prepare:

1. Preheat your oven to 350°F.
2. Arrange a wire rack in a large-sized roasting pan.
3. With the tip of a knife, score the skin of the duck on the breast in a diamond pattern.
4. Rub the duck with salt generously, inside and out.
5. Fill the cavity of the duck with the lemon and garlic slices and tie up the duck legs.
6. Arrange the duck into the prepared roasting pan, breast side up.
7. Roast for 1 hour.
8. Flip the duck and roast for 40 minutes.
9. Remove the roasting pan from oven and transfer the duck onto a platter.
10. Discard the duck juices from the roasting pan.
11. Again, arrange the duck into the roasting pan again, breast side up.
12. In a small-sized bowl, blend together 3 tablespoons of vinegar and ¼ cup of honey.
13. Brush the whole duck with honey mixture evenly and roast for 40 minutes.
14. Meanwhile, in the bowl of glaze, add remaining vinegar, honey, and lemon juice, mix well.
15. Brush the duck with honey mixture evenly and roast for 40 minutes more, brushing with the remaining honey mixture after every 10 minutes.
16. Check if the internal temperature of the meat is above 165°F.
17. Remove the roasting pan from oven and place the duck onto a large serving platter for about 10-15 minutes before carving.
18. Cut the duck into desired-sized pieces and serve.

Nutritional Values:

Calories 489, Total Fat 25.4 g, Saturated Fat 9.5 g, Cholesterol 202 mg, Sodium 161 mg, Total Carbs 8.4 g, Fiber 0.1 g, Sugar 7.9 g, Protein 53.4 g

Stuffed Goose

Preparation time: 15 minutes

Cooking time: 2 hours

Total time: 2¼ hours

Servings: 24

Ingredients:

- 1 (12-pound) goose, neck and giblets removed
- Salt and ground black pepper, as required
- 2 cups carrots, scrubbed and cut in half
- 2 cups celery stalks, cut in half
- 1 head garlic, cut in half crosswise
- 1 bunch fresh thyme
- 1 bunch fresh sage

How to Prepare:

1. Preheat your oven to 400°F.
2. Arrange a wire rack in a large-sized roasting pan.
3. With the point of a sharp knife, prick the entire surface of the goose skin.
4. Carefully fold the neck flap under the body of the goose, and then pin the flap down with a wooden toothpick.
5. Rub the cavity of the goose with salt and black pepper generously.
6. Insert carrots, celery, garlic, thyme, and sage into the cavity of the goose.
7. With kitchen twine, tie the legs together.
8. With your hands, rub the outside of the goose with salt and black pepper generously.
9. Arrange the goose into the prepared roasting pan, breast-side up.
10. Roast for 1 hour, discarding the fat from the roasting pan after every 30 minutes.
11. Now, set the temperature of oven to 325°F and roast for 1 hour further.
12. Check that the internal temperature of the meat is above 165°F.
13. Remove the roasting pan from oven and place the goose onto a large serving platter for about 15-20 minutes before carving.
14. Cut the goose into desired-sized pieces and serve.

Nutritional Values:

Calories 847, Total Fat 76 g, Saturated Fat 22 g, Cholesterol 180 mg, Sodium 191 mg, Total Carbs 1.6 g, Fiber 0.4 g, Sugar 0.6 g, Protein 36.2 g

Crusted Rib Roast

Preparation time: 15 minutes

Cooking time: 2 hours

Total time: 2¼ hours

Servings: 8

Ingredients:

- 4 pounds beef rib roast
- Salt and ground black pepper, as required
- 2 tablespoons olive oil
- 2 tablespoons butter, melted
- 3 medium garlic cloves, minced
- ¼ cup Romano cheese, grated
- 1 cup plain breadcrumbs
- ½ cup fresh parsley, minced

How to Prepare:

1. Preheat your oven to 325°F.
2. Arrange a roasting rack in a large baking dish.
3. Rub the rib roast with salt and black pepper evenly.
4. In a large-sized bowl, blend together oil, butter, and garlic
5. Add rib roast and coat with garlic mixture evenly.
6. In another bowl, blend together cheese, breadcrumbs, and parsley.
7. Transfer the roast to the other bowl and cover with the cheese mixture evenly, pressing gently.
8. Arrange the roast into the prepared baking dish.
9. Roast for approximately 2 hours or until desired doneness.
10. Remove the dish from the oven and place roast onto a cutting board for about 10 minutes.
11. Cut into desired-sized slices and serve.

Nutritional Values:

Calories 607, Total Fat 32.5 g, Saturated Fat 12.6 g, Cholesterol 192 mg, Sodium 364mg, Total Carbs 10.3 g, Fiber 0.8 g, Sugar 0.9 g, Protein 64.8 g

Beef Tenderloin

Preparation time: 15 minutes

Cooking time: 45 minutes

Total time: 1 hour

Servings: 8

Ingredients:

- 2 garlic cloves, sliced thinly
- 2 tablespoons fresh rosemary leaves, minced
- 2-3 fresh rosemary sprigs
- Salt and ground black pepper, as required
- 1 tablespoon vegetable oil
- 3 tablespoons unsalted butter
- 1 (4-pound) center-cut beef tenderloin, trimmed and cut into 2 portions

How to Prepare:

1. Mash the garlic into a paste.
2. In a small-sized bowl, blend together the garlic paste and minced rosemary.
3. Season the roast portions with salt and black pepper generously and then rub with garlic paste mixture.
4. With kitchen twine, tie the tenderloin portions at 1-inch spaces.
5. Arrange the tenderloin portions onto a rimmed baking sheet and refrigerate for about 12 hours.
6. Remove the tenderloin portions from refrigerator and set aside at room temperature for about 2 hours before roasting.
7. Preheat oven to 250°F.
8. Heat vegetable oil in a large oven-proof wok over medium-high heat and cook the tenderloin portions for about 8-10 minutes, flipping occasionally.
9. Immediately, transfer the wok into the oven and roast for 30 minutes, flipping after every 10 minutes.
10. Remove wok from the oven and place the tenderloin portions onto a cutting board for about 10 minutes.
11. Meanwhile, melt butter in a medium-sized frying pan over medium heat and cook the rosemary sprigs for about 4-5 minutes, stirring frequently.
12. Remove the frying pan of butter mixture from heat and discard the rosemary.
13. Untie the tenderloin portions and cut each into desired-sized slices.
14. Drizzle with rosemary butter and serve.

Nutritional Values:

Calories 524, Total Fat 26.9 g, Saturated Fat 11 g, Cholesterol 220 mg, Sodium 184 mg, Total Carbs 0.8 g, Fiber 0.4 g, Sugar 0 g, Protein 65.8 g

Spiced Lamb Shoulder

Preparation time: 15 minutes

Cooking time: 3 hours 35 minutes

Total time: 3 hours 50 minutes

Servings: 14

Ingredients:

- 1 (6-7-pound) bone-in lamb shoulder
- Salt and ground black pepper, as required
- 2 tablespoons coriander seeds
- 2 tablespoons black peppercorns
- 2 tablespoons paprika
- 2 teaspoons ground cinnamon
- 1 teaspoon ground cardamom
- 1 teaspoon ground cloves
- 1 teaspoons nutmeg, grated freshly

How to Prepare:

1. Rub the lamb shoulder with salt and black pepper generously.
2. Arrange the lam shoulder onto a wire rack, arranged inside a rimmed baking sheet.
3. Heat a small, dry wok over medium heat and toast the coriander seeds and peppercorns for about 3 minutes, tossing occasionally.
4. Remove the frying pan from the heat and set aside to cool.
5. In a spice mill, add toasted coriander seeds and peppercorns and grind until finely powdered.
6. Transfer the spice mixture into a small bowl and mix in remaining spices.
7. Rub the lamb shoulder with spice mixture generously.
8. Refrigerate for at least 4 hours.
9. Remove the baking sheet of lamb from oven and set aside at room temperature for about 1 hour before roasting.
10. Preheat your oven to 275°F.
11. Arrange a rack in the middle portion of the oven.
12. Arrange the lamb shoulder into a roasting pan and pour in 3 cups of water.
13. With a piece of foil, cover the roasting pan tightly and roast for approximately 3-3½ hours.
14. While roasting, flip the shoulder and rotate the pan once halfway through.
15. Remove the roasting pan from oven and set the oven to broiler.
16. Remove the foil and discard the liquid from pan.
17. Broil the lamb shoulder for about 5 minutes or until browned.
18. Remove the roasting pan from oven and place the lamb shoulder onto a cutting board for about 20 minutes.
19. Cut into desired-sized slices and serve.

Nutritional Values:

Calories 714, Total Fat 46 g, Saturated Fat 22.9 g, Cholesterol 240 mg, Sodium 184 mg, Total Carbs 1.1 g, Fiber 0.7 g, Sugar 0.2 g, Protein 68.6 g

Herbed Leg of Lamb

Preparation time: 15 minutes

Cooking time: 1¾ hours

Total time: 2 hours

Servings: 12

Ingredients:

- 1 (5-pound) bone-in leg of lamb, trimmed
- 1 tablespoon olive oil
- 1 tablespoon Dijon mustard
- 4 garlic cloves, minced
- 1 tablespoon fresh thyme leaves, chopped
- 1 tablespoon fresh rosemary, chopped
- Salt and ground black pepper, as required

How to Prepare:

1. Preheat your oven to 350°F.
2. Arrange a wire rack into a foil-lined roasting pan.
3. With a sharp knife, score the top side of the lamb with shallow cuts.
4. In a small-sized bowl, blend together the oil, mustard, garlic, herbs, salt and black pepper.
5. Rub the leg of lamb with garlic mixture generously.
6. Arrange the leg of lamb into the prepared roasting pan, fat side up.
7. Roast for approximately 1½-1¾ hours or until desired doneness.
8. Remove the roasting pan from oven and place the leg of lamb onto a cutting board for about 15 minutes.
9. Cut into desired-sized pieces and serve.

Nutritional Values:

Calories 764, Total Fat 52.2 g, Saturated Fat 24.2 g, Cholesterol 267 mg, Sodium 247 mg, Total Carbs 0.9 g, Fiber 0.3 g, Sugar 0 g, Protein 66.9 g

Spiced Pork Shoulder

Preparation time: 15 minutes

Cooking time: 10 hours

Total time: 10¼ hours

Servings: 12

Ingredients:

- ¼ cup black
- peppercorns
- 3 tablespoons juniper berries
- 1 tablespoon coriander seeds
- 3 tablespoons sugar
- Salt, as required
- 10 whole garlic cloves, lightly crushed
- 5 fresh rosemary sprigs
- 2 cups dry white wine
- 2 cups water
- 1 (8-pound) skin-on, bone-in pork shoulder

How to Prepare:

1. In a spice mill, add peppercorns, juniper berries, and coriander seeds and grind until finely powdered.
2. Transfer the spice mixture into a small bowl and mix in the sugar and salt.
3. With a sharp paring knife, cut long parallel lines into the skin of the pork shoulder.
4. Rub the shoulder with spice mixture generously.
5. With plastic wrap, cover the shoulder tightly and refrigerate for at least 3 hours.
6. Preheat your oven to 225°F.
7. Arrange an oven rack in lower third portion of the oven.
8. Line a baking dish with 2 layers of heavy-duty foil.
9. Arrange the garlic cloves and rosemary sprigs in the center of the prepared baking dish.
10. Now, arrange a wire rack on top.
11. Place the pork shoulder over the rack and pour in wine and water.
12. Roast for approximately 9-10 hours.
13. Remove the baking dish from oven and place the pork shoulder onto a cutting board for about 20 minutes.
14. Cut into desired-sized slices and serve.

Nutritional Values:

Calories 824, Total Fat 61.6 g, Saturated Fat 21.4 g, Cholesterol 214 mg, Sodium 215mg, Total Carbs 4.9 g, Fiber 0.1 g, Sugar 3.3 g, Protein 51.1 g

Honey Glazed Ham

Preparation time: 15 minutes

Cooking time: 1¼ hours

Total time: 1½ hours

Servings: 15

Ingredients:

- 1 (5-pound) ready to eat ham
- ¼ cup whole cloves
- 2 cups honey
- ¼ cup dark corn syrup
- 2/3 cup butter

How to Prepare:

1. Preheat your oven to 325°F.
2. Line a large-sized roasting pan with a piece of foil.
3. With a sharp knife, make small slits into the whole ham.
4. Insert the cloves inside the slits.
5. Arrange the ham in the prepared roasting pan.
6. In a microwave-safe bowl, add honey, corn syrup, and butter and microwave on High for about 1½-2 minutes, stirring after every 30 seconds.
7. Remove the bowl of honey mixture from microwave and stir until smooth.
8. Brush the ham with honey glaze generously.
9. Roast for approximately 70 minutes, coating with honey mixture after every 15 minutes.
10. Now, turn the oven to broiler and broil for about 5 minutes or until the glaze is caramelized.
11. Remove the roasting pan of ham from oven and set aside for about 5-10 minutes before slicing.
12. Cut the ham into desired-sized slices and serve.

Nutritional Values:

Calories 476, Total Fat 21.5g, Saturated Fat 9.7 g, Cholesterol 109 mg, Sodium 1087 mg, Total Carbs 48 g, Fiber 2.61 g, Sugar 38.5 g, Protein 25.4 g

TURKEY RECIPES

Fall calls for turkey and these recipes will ensure you cook the best possible bird. Whether it's a Holiday meal or a normal evening, these recipes will help your turkey taste like a masterpiece.

Glazed Turkey Breast 33
Stuffed Turkey Breast 34
Grilled Whole Turkey 36
Turkey & Sweet Potato Chili 38
Turkey & Veggie Pot Pie 40
Turkey Cordon Bleu Casserole 42
Turkey & Pumpkin Pasta 44
Turkey Meatloaf 46
Turkey Pinwheels 48
Turkey & Cranberry Burgers 50

Glazed Turkey Breast

Preparation time: 10 minutes

Cooking time: 2 hours

Total time: 2 hours 10 minutes

Servings: 10

Ingredients:

- ½ cup orange marmalade
- ¼ cup balsamic vinegar
- Salt and ground black pepper, as required
- 1 (5-pound) bone-in turkey breast

How to Prepare:

1. Preheat your oven to 325°F.
2. Arrange a rack in a large baking dish.
3. In a bowl, combine the marmalade, vinegar, salt, and black pepper.
4. Arrange the turkey breast into the prepared baking dish.
5. Bake for approximately 1½-2 hours, brushing with the glaze after every 30 minutes.
6. Remove the baking dish from oven and place the turkey breast onto a cutting board for about 10 minutes.
7. Cut into desired-sized slices and serve.

Nutritional Values:

Calories 481, Total Fat 20.2 g, Saturated Fat 0 g, Cholesterol 177 mg,

Sodium 411 mg, Total Carbs 13.3 g, Fiber 0.1 g, Sugar 12 g, Protein 60.8 g

Stuffed Turkey Breast

Preparation time: 25 minutes

Cooking time: 1 hour 32 minutes

Total time: 1 hour 57 minutes

Servings: 6

Ingredients:

Stuffing

- 5 ounces whole-wheat French bread, cubed
- ½ tablespoon butter
- 1 large celery stalk, minced
- ½ of a medium onion, minced
- ¼ cup fresh parsley, chopped
- 4 fresh sage leaves, minced
- ½ teaspoon poultry seasoning
- Salt and ground black pepper, as required
- 1 large egg, beaten
- ¾ cups chicken broth
- 2 tablespoons dried cranberries, chopped

Turkey Breast

- 1 (2½-pound) skin-on, boneless turkey breast
- Salt, as required
- 1 teaspoon salted butter, softened

How to Prepare:

1. Preheat your oven to 250°F.
2. For stuffing: arrange the bread cubes onto a baking sheet in a single layer.
3. Bake for approximately 30 minutes, stirring once halfway through.
4. Meanwhile, in a large-sized non-stick wok, melt butter over medium-low heat and cook the celery, onion, parsley, sage, poultry seasoning, salt, and black pepper for about 8-10 minutes, stirring frequently.
5. Remove the pan of onion mixture from heat and transfer into a large bowl.
6. Set aside to cool slightly.
7. Add the toasted bread cubes and cranberries, egg, and broth and mix well.
8. Preheat your oven to 375°F.
9. Arrange a rack in the center portion of the oven.
10. For turkey breast: with a sharp paring knife and your fingers, remove the skin from the turkey breast in one piece. Keep the skin.
11. Trim the fat off the breast and remove the tenderloin.
12. Arrange the turkey breast onto a cutting board.
13. Using a knife parallel to the board, cut the breast at the thickest part but not all the way through.
14. Unfold the breast to open it like a book.
15. With plastic wrap, cover the breast and with a meat mallet, pound to ¼-inch thickness.
16. Season both sides of turkey breast with salt evenly.
17. Spread the stuffing onto the turkey breast, leaving about ¾-inch border around all the edges.
18. Then roll the breast in a jelly roll style and top with the skin.
19. With 4-6 pieces of kitchen twine, tie the breast to keep it together.
20. Rub the top of the breast with the butter.
21. Arrange the breast into a baking dish and cover with a piece of foil tightly.
22. Bake for approximately 45-55 minutes.
23. Remove the baking dish with the turkey breast and set the oven to broiler.
24. Remove the foil and broil for about 5-7 minutes.
25. Remove the baking dish from the oven and place the turkey roll onto a cutting board for about 10 minutes.
26. Untie the turkey roll and cut into desired-size slices.
27. Serve immediately.

Nutritional Values:

Calories 276, Total Fat 4.4 g, Saturated Fat 1.9 g, Cholesterol 155 mg,

Sodium 361 mg, Total Carbs 13.4 g, Fiber 2 g, Sugar 0.7 g, Protein 48.9 g

Grilled Whole Turkey

Preparation time: 15 minutes

Cooking time: 2¾ hours

Total time: 3 hours

Servings: 16

Ingredients:

- 2 tablespoons fresh sage, chopped
- 2 tablespoons fresh basil, chopped
- 2 tablespoons vegetable oil
- 2 tablespoons celery salt
- 2 tablespoons ground black pepper
- 1 (12-ounce) jar honey
- 1 (12-pound) whole turkey, giblets and neck removed
- ½ pound mesquite wood chips, soaked in water

How to Prepare:

1. Preheat the grill to high heat.
2. In a bowl, blend together herbs, oil, celery salt, and black pepper.
3. In a large-sized roasting pan, arrange turkey, breast side down.
4. Coat the turkey with herb mixture generously.
5. Using a piece of foil, cover the turkey.
6. Arrange the roasting pan over the grill grate.
7. Immediately throw a handful of the soaked wood chips on the fire and cover the grill with lid.
8. Cook for about 1 hour.
9. Remove the foil from roasting pan and coat the turkey with half of the honey.
10. Again, wrap the turkey with a piece of foil and cover the grill with lid.
11. Cook for about 1-1½ hours.
12. Remove the piece of foil and coat turkey with the remaining honey.
13. Now, place turkey, breast side up.
14. Cook uncovered for about 15 minutes.
15. Remove from grill and set aside for 15 minutes before serving.
16. Cut into desired-sized pieces and serve.

Nutritional Values:

Calories 661, Total Fat 18.8 g, Saturated Fat 6 g, Cholesterol 258 mg, Sodium 243 mg, Total Carbs 18.3 g, Fiber 0.4 g, Sugar 17.5 g, Protein 99.8 g

Turkey & Sweet Potato Chili

Preparation time: 15 minutes

Cooking time: 7 hours 10 minutes

Total time: 7 hours 25 minutes

Servings: 4

Ingredients:

- 2 sweet potatoes, peeled and chopped
- ¾ cup sweet onion, chopped
- ½ cup celery stalk, chopped
- 2 (14½-ounce) cans diced tomatoes with chili seasoning
- 1 (8-ounce) can tomato sauce
- ½ cup water
- 1 tablespoon red chili powder
- ½ teaspoon ground cinnamon
- ½ teaspoon ground cumin
- ¼ teaspoon onion powder
- ¼ teaspoon garlic powder
- Salt and ground black pepper, as required
- 1 pound ground turkey
- 1 cup corn
- 1 (14-ounce) can white beans

How to Prepare:

1. Heat a large-sized non-stick wok over medium-high heat and cook turkey for about 8-10 minutes.
2. Remove the wok with the turkey from heat and drain the excess fat from the wok.
3. In a slow cooker, add the cooked turkey, sweet potato, onion, celery, tomatoes, tomato sauce, water, and spices and mix well.
4. With the lid, cover the slow cooker and set on High for 5 hours, stirring occasionally.
5. Uncover the slow cooker and add in the corn and beans (drained and rinsed).
6. Again, cover the slow cooker and set on High for 1-2 hours further.
7. Serve hot.

Nutritional Values:

Calories 508, Total Fat 14.8 g, Saturated Fat 2.4 g, Cholesterol 116 mg, Sodium 743 mg, Total Carbs 58.4 g, Fiber 17.9 g, Sugar 11.5 g, Protein 44.8 g

Turkey & Veggie Pot Pie

Preparation time: 15 minutes

Cooking time: 1 hour

Total time: 1¼ hours

Servings: 6

Ingredients:

- 1 single pastry pie crust
- 4 cups cooked turkey meat, cubed
- 1 (10¾-ounce) can condensed cream of chicken soup
- 2 cups water, divided
- 1 (16-ounce) package mixed frozen vegetables
- 2 (1½-ounce) packages turkey gravy mix
- 4 cups boiled potatoes, peeled and mashed

How to Prepare:

1. Preheat your oven to 375°F.
2. Arrange the pie crust in the bottom of a 13x9-inch baking dish and gently press down.
3. Place the cooked turkey meat over the crust evenly.
4. Pour cream of chicken soup over turkey meat evenly.
5. In a pan, add 1 cup of water over medium heat and bring to a boil.
6. Add in the vegetables and cook for about 5 minutes.
7. In a bowl, add remaining water and turkey gravy mix and stir to combine.
8. Add gravy mixture into the pan of vegetables and bring to boil.
9. Cook for about 1 minute, stirring continuously.
10. Now, place the vegetable mixture over turkey and soup layer.
11. Top with mashed potatoes evenly.
12. Bake for approximately 45 minutes.
13. Remove the baking dish of pot pie from oven and set aside for about 5 minutes before serving.

Nutritional Values:

Calories 418, Total Fat 6.7 g, Saturated Fat 2.1 g, Cholesterol 74 mg, Sodium 938 mg, Total Carbs 53.5 g, Fiber 7 g, Sugar 4.9 g, Protein 34.2 g

Turkey Cordon Bleu Casserole

Preparation time: 15 minutes

Cooking time: 30 minutes

Total time: 55 minutes

Servings: 8

Ingredients:

- 2 cups uncooked elbow macaroni
- 2 (10¾-) cans condensed cream of chicken soup, undiluted
- ¾ cup milk
- ¼ cup Parmesan cheese, grated
- 2 cups part-skim mozzarella cheese, shredded
- 1 teaspoon mustard
- ½ teaspoon dried rosemary, crushed
- 1 teaspoon paprika
- ¼ teaspoon garlic powder
- 1/8 teaspoon ground sage
- 2 cups cooked turkey, cubed
- 2 cups fully cooked ham, cubed
- ¼ cup Ritz crackers, crushed

How to Prepare:

1. Preheat your oven to 350°F.
2. Grease a 13x9-inch casserole dish.
3. In a large-sized saucepan of lightly salted boiling water, cook the macaroni for about 8-10 minutes.
4. Drain the macaroni and set aside.
5. In a bowl, add soup, milk, Parmesan cheese, mustard, rosemary, and spices and beat until well blended.
6. Add the cooked macaroni, turkey, ham, and mozzarella and mix well.
7. In a casserole dish, place mixture, spread evenly and sprinkle with crackers.
8. Bake for approximately 26-30 minutes or until golden brown and bubbly.
9. Remove the casserole from oven and set aside for about 5 minutes before serving.

Nutritional Values:

Calories 289, Total Fat 9.5 g, Saturated Fat 3.7 g, Cholesterol 56 mg, Sodium 855 mg, Total Carbs 26.1 g, Fiber 2 g, Sugar 2.3 g, Protein 23.9 g

Turkey & Pumpkin Pasta

Preparation time: 15 minutes

Cooking time: 35 minutes

Total time: 50 minutes

Servings: 4

Ingredients:

- 1 (32-ounce) carton chicken broth
- 2 tablespoons olive oil
- 1 cup onion, chopped finely
- 1 teaspoon fresh thyme, chopped finely
- ¾ pound dried small pasta
- Salt and ground black pepper, as required
- 1 cup cooked turkey, cubed
- 1 cup pumpkin puree
- ½ cup Parmesan cheese, grated freshly plus extra for garnishing

How to Prepare:

1. In a saucepan, cook broth over medium-high heat and bring to a boil.
2. Now adjust the heat to low and let the soup simmer.
3. Meanwhile, in another saucepan, heat oil over medium-high heat and sauté onion for about 2-3 minutes.
4. Add thyme and 2 cups of hot broth and bring to a boil.
5. Add the pasta, salt, and black pepper and stir to combine.
6. Now adjust the heat to low.
7. Pour ½ cup of hot broth at a time after the absorbing of previous broth.
8. While adding broth, stir occasionally and simmer for about 15 minutes.
9. Add turkey and pumpkin puree and stir until well blended.
10. Stir in cheese and cook for about 1-2 minutes or until cheese is melted completely.
11. Serve hot with the topping of extra cheese.

Nutritional Values:

Calories 554, Total Fat 20.2 g, Saturated Fat 7.3 g, Cholesterol 119 mg, Sodium 937 mg, Total Carbs 55.2 g, Fiber 2.5 g, Sugar 3.9 g, Protein 37.3 g

Turkey Meatloaf

Preparation time: 15 minutes

Cooking time: 1 hour

Total time: 1 hour 20 minutes

Servings: 6

Ingredients:

Meatloaf

- 1 pound lean ground turkey
- 8 ounces bacon, chopped
- 1 cup carrot, peeled and grated finely
- 3 cups celery stalks, chopped
- 1 brown onion, chopped
- ½ cup almond meal
- 2 teaspoon fresh parsley, minced
- ½ teaspoon cayenne pepper
- Salt and ground black pepper, as required
- 2 eggs, beaten
- 2 tablespoons Worcestershire sauce

Cranberry Glaze

- ½ cup dried cranberries
- 1 teaspoon ground cinnamon
- 2 teaspoons fresh orange zest, grated finely
- 2 tablespoons fresh orange juice
- ½ cup water

How to Prepare:

1. Preheat your oven to 350°F.
2. Line a bread loaf pan with lightly greased baking paper.
3. For meatloaf: in a bowl, add all ingredients and mix until well blended.
4. Place the turkey mixture into the prepared bread pan.
5. Bake for approximately 50 minutes.
6. For the glaze: in a saucepan, add all ingredients over medium heat and bring to a boil.
7. Now, adjust the heat to low and simmer for about 10 minutes, stirring occasionally.
8. Remove the saucepan of glaze from heat and with a hand blender, blend the glaze until chunky puree forms.
9. After 50 minutes of baking, remove the meatloaf from the oven.
10. Top the meatloaf with cranberry glaze.
11. Bake for approximately 10 minutes more.
12. Remove the loaf pan from the oven and set aside for about 10 minutes before slicing.
13. Cut the meatloaf into desired-sized slices and serve.

Nutritional Values:

Calories 417, Total Fat 26.8 g, Saturated Fat 7.7 g, Cholesterol 150 mg, Sodium 937 mg, Total Carbs 10.3 g, Fiber 3.4 g, Sugar 4.6 g, Protein 33.2 g

Turkey Pinwheels

Preparation time: 20 minutes

Cooking time: 1 hour

Total time: 1 hour 20 minutes

Servings: 5

Ingredients:

Meatloaf

- 1¼ pounds ground turkey
- 1 egg, beaten
- ¾ cup soft breadcrumbs
- Salt and ground black pepper, as required

Topping

- 3 tablespoons ketchup
- ¼ cup Italian cheese blend, shredded
- ½ teaspoon Italian seasoning

Filling

- ¾ cup Italian cheese blend, shredded
- 1 (10-ounce) package frozen chopped spinach, thawed completely and drained
- 1 teaspoon Italian seasoning
- Salt and ground black pepper, as required

How to Prepare:

1. Preheat your oven to 350°F.
2. Arrange a rack into a roasting pan.
3. Line a baking sheet with baking paper.
4. For meatloaf: in a bowl, add turkey, egg, breadcrumbs, salt, and black pepper and mix until well blended.
5. Place the turkey mixture onto the prepared baking sheet and shape into a 10x14-inch rectangle.
6. With your hands, slightly pat the mixture.
7. For filling: in a large-sized bowl, add all ingredients and gently mix.
8. Place the spinach mixture over turkey mixture, leaving about ¾-inch space from the sides.
9. Pick up one edge of baking paper and roll it over the meat, starting with the short end.
10. Continue to roll until the meat mixture forms a firm roll by pulling back the baking paper.
11. Place the roll into the prepared roasting pan, seam side down.
12. Bake for approximately 50 minutes.
13. Remove the roasting pan from oven.
14. Spread the ketchup on top evenly and sprinkle with cheese, followed by Italian seasoning.
15. Bake for approximately 10 minutes further.
16. Remove the roasting pan from oven and set aside for about 10 minutes before slicing.
17. Cut the roll into desired-sized slices and serve.

Nutritional Values:

Calories 403, Total Fat 21 g, Saturated Fat 6.5 g, Cholesterol 172 mg, Sodium 604 mg, Total Carbs 16.4 g, Fiber 2 g, Sugar 3.7 g, Protein 42 g

Turkey & Cranberry Burgers

Preparation time: 15 minutes

Cooking time: 12 minutes

Total time: 27 minutes

Servings: 6

Ingredients:

- 3 tablespoons boiling water
- 1 white bread slice, torn into small chunks
- 1 garlic clove, minced
- 1 pound ground turkey
- ¼ cup dried cranberries, chopped
- ½ of medium red onion, chopped
- 2 fresh rosemary sprigs, chopped
- 2 tablespoons tomato ketchup
- 2 ounces Brie cheese, cubed
- Salt and ground black pepper, as required

How to Prepare:

1. Preheat your oven to broiler.
2. Arrange a rack in the oven about 6-inches from the top heating element.
3. In a large-sized bowl, add water, bread slice, and garlic.
4. With a fork, mash the slice completely.
5. Add remaining ingredients and blend well.
6. Make 6 equal-sized patties from the mixture.
7. Arrange the patties onto a broiler pan.
8. Broil for about 6 minutes per side.
9. Serve hot.

Nutritional Values:

Calories 202, Total Fat 11.1 g, Saturated Fat 3.1 g, Cholesterol 87 mg, Sodium 252 mg, Total Carbs 4.9 g, Fiber 0.5 g, Sugar 1.9 g, Protein 23.2 g

WARM POULTRY DISHES

Everyone loves a warm, comforting poultry dinner during the coldest months of the year. Keep your spirits high with these delicious meals for holidays or every day.

Cheesy Buffalo Chicken	52
Chicken Roulade	54
Chicken with Butternut Squash	56
Chicken with Pears	58
Chicken & Pumpkin Curry	60
Chicken in Orange Sauce	62
Chicken in Fig Sauce	64
Stuffed Cornish Hens	66
Pesto Chicken Bake	68
Chicken in Cranberry Sauce	69

Cheesy Buffalo Chicken

Preparation time: 15 minutes

Cooking time: 18 minutes

Total time: 33 minutes

Servings: 4

Ingredients:

- 4 (4-ounce) boneless, skinless chicken breast
- 1 teaspoon garlic powder
- Salt and ground black pepper, as required
- Pinch of cayenne pepper
- 3 tablespoons unsalted butter, divided
- 2 garlic cloves, minced
- 1 cup buffalo sauce
- 8 muenster cheese slices

How to Prepare:

1. Season each chicken breast with garlic powder, salt, and black pepper evenly.
2. In a large wok, melt 1 tablespoon of butter over medium heat and cook the chicken breasts for about 5-7 minutes per side.
3. With a slotted spoon, transfer the cooked chicken breasts onto a plate.
4. In the same wok, melt the remaining butter over medium heat and sauté the garlic for about 1 minute.
5. Add the buffalo sauce and cayenne pepper and stir to combine.
6. Stir in the cooked chicken breasts and top each with 2 cheese slices.
7. Simmer, covered for about 3 minutes.
8. Serve hot.

Nutritional Values:

Calories 392, Total Fat 24.3g, Saturated Fat 13.6 g, Cholesterol 136 mg, Sodium 1037 mg, Total Carbs 4.2 g, Fiber 0.1 g, Sugar 3.3 g, Protein 38 g

Chicken Roulade

Preparation time: 15 minutes

Cooking time: 17 minutes

Total time: 32 minutes

Servings: 4

Ingredients:

- 4 (6-ounce) skinless, boneless chicken breasts, pounded into 1/8-inch thickness
- 4 tablespoons olive oil, divided
- Salt and ground black pepper, as required
- 4 ounces feta cheese, crumbled
- 2 tablespoons fresh oregano, minced
- 4 garlic cloves, minced
- ½ teaspoon lemon zest, grated

How to Prepare:

1. Preheat oven to 450°F.
2. Brush the chicken breasts with 2 tablespoons of oil and then season with salt and black pepper.
3. Arrange the chicken breasts onto a smooth surface.
4. Top each chicken breast with feta, followed by oregano, garlic, and lemon zest, leaving edges.
5. Roll each breast like a jelly roll to seal the filling securely.
6. With kitchen twine, tie each roll at 1-inch intervals.
7. Heat remaining oil and add chickens to cook for about 10 minutes or until browned on all sides.
8. Remove the wok of chicken rolls from heat.
9. Arrange the rolls into a baking dish in a single layer.
10. Bake for approximately 5-7 minutes.
11. Serve hot.

Nutritional Values:

Calories 419, Total Fat 26.4 g, Saturated Fat 8.5 g, Cholesterol 124 mg, Sodium 417 mg, Total Carbs 3.7 g, Fiber 1 g, Sugar 1.3 g, Protein 42.5 g

Chicken with Butternut Squash

Preparation time: 15 minutes

Cooking time: 30 minutes

Total time: 45 minutes

Servings: 4

Ingredients:

- 4 (5-ounce) boneless, skin-on chicken breast halves
- 2 tablespoons olive oil, divided
- 2 tablespoons paprika
- Ground black pepper, as required
- 1 cup apple cider
- 2 tablespoons butter, softened
- 1 tablespoon soy sauce
- 1 tablespoon brown sugar
- 1 tablespoon mustard
- 2 cups butternut squash, cut into ¼-inch cubes
- 1 tablespoon fresh thyme, chopped

How to Prepare:

1. Preheat your oven to 420°F.
2. In a small-sized bowl, combine 1 tablespoon of olive oil, paprika, and black pepper.
3. Rub each chicken breast with oil mixture generously.
4. Set aside for about 15 minutes.
5. Heat an oven-proof wok over medium-high heat.
6. In the wok, place the chicken breasts, skin side down and sear for about 4-5 minutes.
7. Transfer the chicken breasts onto a plate.
8. In the same wok, add apple cider, butter, soy sauce, brown sugar, and mustard and mix well.
9. Place the wok over medium heat and bring to a boil, stirring continuously.
10. Meanwhile, in a large mixing bowl, add butternut squash, thyme, and remaining olive oil and toss to coat.
11. Remove from heat and place the chicken breasts into the wok, skin side up.
12. Place the butternut squash cubes into the wok and spread around the chicken.
13. Bake for approximately 20 minutes.
14. Serve hot.

Nutritional Values:

Calories 421, Total Fat 18.5 g, Saturated Fat 6 g, Cholesterol 124 mg, Sodium 353 mg, Total Carbs 21,3 g, Fiber 3.4 g, Sugar 11.1 g, Protein 43.4 g

Chicken with Pears

Preparation time: 15 minutes

Cooking time: 25 minutes

Total time: 40 minutes

Servings: 4

Ingredients:

- 1 cup chicken broth
- 2 tablespoons apple cider vinegar
- 2 teaspoons tapioca flour
- 2 tablespoons extra-virgin olive oil
- 4 garlic cloves, minced
- 2 tablespoons fresh basil, minced
- 4 (4-ounce) skinless, boneless chicken breasts
- Salt and ground black pepper, as required
- 2 Bosc pears, cored and sliced

How to Prepare:

1. In a bowl, blend together the broth, vinegar, and tapioca starch. Keep aside.
2. In a large-sized cast-iron wok, heat oil over medium-high heat and sauté garlic and basil for about 1 minute.
3. Add chicken, salt, and black pepper and cook for about 12-15 minutes.
4. Transfer the chicken into a bowl.
5. In the same wok, add the pears and cook for about 4-5 minutes.
6. Add the broth mixture and bring to a boil.
7. Cook for about 1 minute.
8. Add the chicken and stir to combine.
9. Now adjust the heat to low and cook for about 3-4 minutes.
10. Serve hot.

Nutritional Values:

Calories 284, Total Fat 11.6 g, Saturated Fat 2.6 g, Cholesterol 66 mg, Sodium 272 mg, Total Carbs 18.7 g, Fiber 3.3 g, Sugar 10.5 g, Protein 27.1 g

Chicken & Pumpkin Curry

Preparation time: 15 minutes

Cooking time: 35 minutes

Total time: 50 minutes

Servings: 4

Ingredients:

- 14 ounces chicken breast, cut into small cubes
- 1 teaspoon poultry seasoning
- 1 tablespoon olive oil
- 1 tablespoon butter
- 1 onion, chopped
- 1 (1-inch) piece fresh ginger, chopped finely
- 2 garlic cloves, minced
- 1 tablespoon ground cumin
- 1 tablespoon ground cumin
- 1 teaspoon red pepper flakes, crushed
- Pinch of ground turmeric
- 1 (2-pound) sugar pumpkin, peeled, seeded and cubed
- 1½ cups chicken broth
- ½ cup canned coconut milk
- Salt, as required

How to Prepare:

1. Coat the chicken with poultry seasoning completely and set aside for about 5 minutes.
2. In a large-sized cast-iron wok, heat oil over medium heat and cook the chicken pieces for about 4-5 minutes or until cooked.
3. Transfer the cooked chicken pieces into a bowl and set aside.
4. In the same wok, melt butter over medium heat and sauté onion for about 3-4 minutes.
5. Add ginger, garlic, and spices and sauté for about 1 minute.
6. Stir in pumpkin, broth, coconut milk, and cooked chicken and bring to a boil.
7. Immediately cover the wok and cook for about 15-20 minutes or until desired thickness.
8. Season with salt and remove from heat.
9. Serve hot.

Nutritional Values:

Calories 344, Total Fat 18.2 g, Saturated Fat 3.2 g, Cholesterol 57 mg, Sodium 396 mg, Total Carbs 24.6 g, Fiber 8.2 g, Sugar 10 g, Protein 24.8 g

Chicken in Orange Sauce

Preparation time: 15 minutes

Cooking time: 20 minutes

Total time: 35 minutes

Servings: 6

Ingredients:

- 1 teaspoon fresh ginger, minced
- ½ cup fresh orange juice
- 1 tablespoon apple cider vinegar
- 2 tablespoons low-sodium soy sauce
- ¼ teaspoon ground cinnamon
- Ground black pepper, as required
- 2 pounds skinless, bone-in chicken thighs

How to Prepare:

1. For marinade: in a large-sized bowl, add all the ingredients except for chicken thighs and mix well.
2. In the bowl, add the chicken thighs and coat with the marinade generously.
3. Cover the bowl and refrigerate to marinate for about 2 hours.
4. Remove the chicken thighs from the bowl, reserving marinade.
5. Heat a large-sized non-stick wok over medium-high heat and cook the chicken for about 5-6 minutes or until golden brown.
6. Flip the side and cook for about 4 minutes.
7. Add the marinade and bring to a boil.
8. Now adjust the heat to medium-low and cook, covered for about 6-8 minutes or until sauce becomes thick.
9. Serve hot.

Nutritional Values:

Calories 300, Total Fat 11.3 g, Saturated Fat 3.1 g, Cholesterol 135 mg, Sodium 424 mg, Total Carbs 2.8 g, Fiber 0.1 g, Sugar 2.1 g, Protein 44.2 g

Chicken in Fig Sauce

Preparation time: 15 minutes

Cooking time: 20 minutes

Total time: 35 minutes

Servings: 4

Ingredients:

- 4 (6-ounce) skinless, boneless chicken breast halves
- 1½ tablespoons fresh thyme, chopped and divided
- ½ teaspoon salt, divided
- ¼ teaspoon ground black pepper
- 2 tablespoons olive oil, divided
- ¾ cup onion, chopped
- ½ cup dried figs, chopped finely
- ½ cup low-sodium chicken broth
- ¼ cup balsamic vinegar
- 2 teaspoons low-sodium soy sauce

How to Prepare:

1. In a small-sized bowl, add 1½ teaspoons of thyme, ¼ teaspoon of salt and black pepper and mix well.
2. Season the chicken breast halves with the thyme mixture evenly.
3. In a large-sized cast-iron wok, heat 1 tablespoon of the oil over medium-high heat.
4. In the wok, place the chicken breasts, skin side down and cook for about 5-6 minutes per side.
5. With a slotted spoon, transfer the cooked chicken breasts onto a plate and with a piece of foil, cover them to keep warm.
6. Heat remaining 1 tablespoon of the oil in the same wok over medium heat and sauté the onion for about 3 minutes.
7. Stir in the figs, broth, vinegar, and soy sauce and simmer for about 3 minutes.
8. Stir in the remaining thyme and salt and remove from the heat.
9. Cut the chicken breast halves into slices diagonally.
10. Serve the chicken with the topping of fig sauce.

Nutritional Values:

Calories 352, Total Fat 13.4 g, Saturated Fat 3.4 g, Cholesterol 99 mg, Sodium 512 mg, Total Carbs 19.1 g, Fiber 3.3 g, Sugar 13.1 g, Protein 39.6g

Stuffed Cornish Hens

Preparation time: 15 minutes

Cooking time: 1 hour

Total time: 1¼ hour

Servings: 12

Ingredients:

- 1 tablespoon dried basil, crushed
- 2 tablespoon lemon pepper
- 1 tablespoon poultry seasoning
- Salt, as required
- 2 tablespoons olive oil
- 1 large onion, chopped
- 2 medium celery stalks, chopped
- 1 bell pepper, seeded and chopped
- 6 (1½-pound) Cornish game hens

How to Prepare:

1. Preheat your oven to 375°F.
2. Arrange 1 rack in each of 2 large-sized roasting pans.
3. In a bowl, blend together basil, lemon pepper, salt, and poultry seasoning.
4. Coat the hens with oil and rub with the seasoning mixture evenly.
5. In a bowl, blend together vegetables.
6. Stuff the cavities of hens with veggie mixture loosely.
7. Arrange hens into prepared roasting pans, keeping plenty of space between them.
8. Roast for approximately 58-60 minutes or until juices run clear.
9. Check the internal temperature of the meat to ensure it is above 165°F.
10. Remove the hens from oven and transfer onto the serving plates.
11. With a piece of foil, cover each hen for about 10 minutes before serving.

Nutritional Values:

Calories 700, Total Fat 51 g, Saturated Fat 0.4 g, Cholesterol 349 mg, Sodium 226mg, Total Carbs 2.8 g, Fiber 0.7 g, Sugar 1.1 g, Protein 58.1 g

Pesto Chicken Bake

Preparation time: 15 minutes

Cooking time: 42 minutes

Total time: 57 minutes

Servings: 4

Ingredients:

- 4 (4-ounce) boneless, skinless chicken breast halves
- ½ cup basil pesto
- 2 plum tomatoes, sliced
- 1 cup mozzarella cheese, shredded

How to Prepare:

1. Preheat your oven to 400°F.
2. Line baking sheet with a greased piece of foil.
3. In a bowl, add the chicken breasts and pesto and toss to coat well.
4. Place the coated chicken breast halves onto the prepared baking sheet in a single layer.
5. Bake for 35 minutes.
6. Remove from the oven and top the chicken breasts with the tomato slices, followed by the cheese.
7. Bake for approximately 5-7 minutes or until cheese melts completely.
8. Serve hot.

Nutritional Values:

Calories 161, Total Fat 4.2 g, Saturated Fat 0.8 g, Cholesterol 76 mg, Sodium 103 mg, Total Carbs 2.7 g, Fiber 0.8 g, Sugar 1.6 g, Protein 26.4 g

Chicken in Cranberry Sauce

Preparation time: 10 minutes

Cooking time: 1 hour 45 minutes

Total time: 1 hour 55 minutes

Servings: 6

Ingredients:

- 1 (8-ounce) bottle Russian-style salad dressing
- 1 (16-ounce) can cranberry sauce
- 1 package dry onion soup mix
- 6 (5-6-ounce) chicken thighs

How to Prepare:

1. Preheat your oven to 350°F.
2. Lightly grease a 13x9-inch baking dish.
3. In a large-sized bowl, blend together all ingredients except for the thighs.
4. Add thighs and coat with sauce mixture generously.
5. Place the chicken thigh mixture into the prepared baking dish and then arrange them in a single layer.
6. Cover baking dish and bake 1½ hours approximately.
7. Uncover the baking dish and bake for approximately 15 minutes.
8. Serve hot.

Nutritional Values:

Calories 459, Total Fat 20.4 g, Saturated Fat 4.5 g, Cholesterol 126 mg, Sodium 857 mg, Total Carbs 21.7 g, Fiber 3.9g, Sugar 11.1 g, Protein 42 g

MEAT MAINS

Protein is incredibly important for providing your body with the proper amount of iron needed. Meat also helps keep you warm in the winter by improving blood flow. These meat mains are not only good for your body but also good for your soul.

GLAZED FILET MIGNON	71
BEEF STROGANOFF	72
BEEF WELLINGTON	74
SHEPHERD'S PIE	76
GLAZED PORK RIBS	78
CRANBERRY & APPLE STUFFED PORK CHOPS	80
SAUSAGE & BACON BREAD CASSEROLE	82
BRAISED LAMB SHANKS	84
PAN-SEARED LAMB CHOPS	86
PORK WITH BRUSSELS SPROUTS	88

Glazed Filet Mignon

Preparation time: 10 minutes

Cooking time: 12 minutes

Total time: 22 minutes

Servings: 2

Ingredients:

- 2 (4-ounce) filet mignon
- Salt and ground black pepper, as required
- ¼ cup red wine
- ¼ cup dry red wine vinegar

How to Prepare:

1. Rub the filets with salt and black pepper generously.
2. Heat a medium non-stick wok over medium-high heat and cook filets for about 1-2 minutes per side or until browned.
3. Add wine and vinegar and immediately adjust the heat to medium-low.
4. Cover and cook for about 4 minutes.
5. Flip the filets and baste with pan sauce.
6. Cover and cook for about 4 minutes more.
7. Transfer the steaks to serving plates.
8. Top with pan glaze and serve immediately.

Nutritional Values:

Calories 266, Total Fat 10.8 g, Saturated Fat 4.1 g, Cholesterol 97 mg, Sodium 153 mg, Total Carbs 1.1 g, Fiber 0 g, Sugar 0.4 g, Protein 32.4 g

Beef Stroganoff

Preparation time: 20 minutes

Cooking time: 1 hour

Total time: 1 hour 20 minutes

Servings: 8

Ingredients:

Beef Stroganoff

- 2 tablespoons olive oil, divided
- 1 teaspoon steak seasoning
- Salt and ground black pepper, as required
- 1 pound fresh cremini mushrooms, quartered
- 1 large yellow onion, chopped finely
- 1½ pound ground beef
- 4 cups cauliflower rice

Sauce

- 1 cup sour cream
- ½ cup mayonnaise
- 1-2 tablespoons beef broth
- 1 cup mozzarella cheese, grated
- ¼ cup parmesan cheese, grated
- ½ teaspoon steak seasoning

Topping

- 1 cup mozzarella cheese
- Grated

How to Prepare:

1. Preheat your oven to 375°F.
2. Grease a large glass casserole dish.
3. For stroganoff: in a large, heavy-bottomed sauté pan, heat 2 teaspoons of oil over medium-high heat and cook the beef for about 4-5 minutes or until browned completely, breaking up the meat.
4. Remove sauté pan from the heat and transfer the browned beef into the prepared casserole dish.
5. In the same sauté pan, add 2 teaspoons of the remaining oil over medium-high heat and cook the mushrooms for about 6-7 minutes.
6. Remove wok from the heat and place the mushrooms into the casserole dish with the beef.
7. In the same sauté pan, heat the remaining oil over medium-high heat and sauté the onion for about 4-5 minutes.
8. Add the cauliflower rice, steak seasoning, salt, and pepper and stir to combine.
9. Now adjust the heat to high and cook for about 3 minutes.
10. Remove from the heat and transfer the onion mixture into the casserole dish with the beef mixture and gently stir to combine.
11. For sauce: in a bowl, add the sour cream, mayonnaise, and broth and mix until well blended.
12. Add mozzarella, parmesan cheese, and steak seasoning and stir to combine.
13. Place the sauce over the beef mixture and gently stir to combine.
14. Place the mozzarella cheese on the top evenly.
15. Bake for approximately 30-40 minutes or until cheese is bubbly.
16. Remove from the oven and serve hot.

Nutritional Values:

Calories 392, Total Fat 23.1 g, Saturated Fat 9 g, Cholesterol 104 mg, Sodium 453 mg, Total Carbs 12.2 g, Fiber 2 g, Sugar 4 g, Protein 35.4 g

Beef Wellington

Preparation time: 20 minutes

Cooking time: 40 minutes

Total time: 1 hour

Servings: 4

Ingredients:

- 2 (4-ounces) beef tenderloin steaks, halved
- Salt and ground black pepper, as required
- 1 tablespoon butter
- 1 cup mozzarella cheese, shredded
- ½ cup almond flour
- 4 tablespoons liver pate

How to Prepare:

1. Preheat your oven to 400°F.
2. Grease a baking sheet.
3. Season each steak half with salt and black pepper evenly.
4. In a medium-sized sauté pan, melt the butter over medium-high heat and sear the beef steaks for about 2-3 minutes per side.
5. Remove the sauté pan from heat and set aside to cool completely.
6. In a microwave-safe bowl, add the mozzarella cheese and microwave for about 1 minute.
7. Remove the bowl of mozzarella from microwave and immediately stir in the almond flour until a dough forms.
8. Place the dough between 2 baking paper pieces and with a rolling pin, roll to flatten it.
9. Remove the upper baking paper piece.
10. Divide the rolled dough into 4 pieces.
11. Place 1 tablespoon of pate onto each dough piece and top with 1 steak piece.
12. Cover each steak piece with dough completely.
13. Arrange the covered steak pieces onto the prepared baking sheet in a single layer.
14. Bake for approximately 22-30 minutes or until the pastry is golden brown.
15. Serve warm.

Nutritional Values:

Calories 276, Total Fat 18 g, Saturated Fat 5.6 g, Cholesterol 95 mg, Sodium 235 mg, Total Carbs 3.5 g, Fiber 1.5 g, Sugar 0 g, Protein 24.1 g

Shepherd's Pie

Preparation time: 20 minutes

Cooking time: 1 hour 5 minutes

Total time: 1 hour 25 minutes

Servings: 8

Ingredients:

- 4-6 bacon slices, chopped
- 2 pounds ground beef
- ½ cup onion, chopped
- ¼ teaspoon garlic powder
- ¼ teaspoon onion powder
- Salt and ground black pepper, as required
- 8 ounces cheddar cheese, shredded and divided
- 1 egg, beaten
- 16 ounces frozen green beans
- 3 tablespoons butter, divided
- 16 ounces frozen cauliflower
- ¼ cup sour cream

How to Prepare:

1. Preheat your oven to 350ºF.
2. Lightly grease a baking dish.
3. Heat a large-sized non-stick sauté pan over medium-high heat and cook bacon for about 8-10 minutes or until crisp.
4. Drain the excess grease from wok.
5. Transfer the bacon into a bowl.
6. In the same sauté pan, add beef and cook for about 4-5 minutes.
7. Add onion and cook for about 4-5 minutes. Drain the excess fats.
8. Stir in garlic powder, onion powder, salt, and black pepper and remove from heat.
9. Stir in ½ of cheese, egg, and cooked bacon and transfer into a baking dish.
10. Meanwhile, in a pan of boiling water, add green beans and cook for about 4-5 minutes.
11. Drain the green beans well and transfer into a bowl.
12. Add 1 tablespoon of butter and some salt and mix.
13. In a pan of boiling water, add cauliflower and boil for about 10-12 minutes.
14. Drain the cauliflower well.
15. In a food processor, add cauliflower, sour cream, remaining butter, and a pinch of salt and black pepper and pulse until smooth.
16. Place green beans over beef mixture evenly.
17. Top with cauliflower mixture evenly.
18. Sprinkle with remaining cheese evenly.
19. Bake for approximately 35 minutes or until bubbly.
20. Serve hot.

Nutritional Values:

Calories 503, Total Fat 29.3 g, Saturated Fat 14.6 g, Cholesterol 183 mg, Sodium 680 mg, Total Carbs 8.8 g, Fiber 3.5 g, Sugar 20.7 g, Protein 50.3 g

Glazed Pork Ribs

Preparation time: 20 minutes

Cooking time: 1 hour 5 minutes

Total time: 1 hour 25 minutes

Servings: 8

Ingredients:

- 2 tablespoons olive oil
- 1 small onion, minced
- 1½ cups honey
- 1 cup Dijon mustard
- ½ cup cider vinegar
- 3 tablespoons red pepper flakes, crushed
- 1 teaspoon Cajun seasoning
- Salt and ground black pepper, as required
- 2 (2-pound) slabs pork baby back ribs

How to Prepare:

1. Preheat the grill to medium heat.
2. Lightly grease the grill grate.
3. In a sauté pan, heat oil over medium heat and sauté onion for about 5 minutes.
4. Add honey, mustard, vinegar, red pepper flakes, Cajun seasoning, salt, and black pepper and stir to combine.
5. Now adjust the heat to low and simmer for about 5 minutes, stirring occasionally.
6. Remove from heat and set aside.
7. Sprinkle ribs with salt and pepper generously.
8. Place ribs onto the grill grate.
9. Cover the grill and open vents halfway.
10. Cook for about 35 minutes, flipping once halfway through.
11. Coat ribs with sauce and cook, covered for about 5-10 minutes per side.
12. Meanwhile, heat the remaining sauce.
13. Remove the ribs from grill and place onto a platter.
14. Top with sauce and serve.

Nutritional Values:

Calories 899, Total Fat 59.33 g, Saturated Fat 20.7 g, Cholesterol 181 mg, Sodium 555 mg, Total Carbs 55.1 g, Fiber 1.9 g, Sugar 53.1 g, Protein 38 g

Cranberry & Apple Stuffed Pork Chops

Preparation time: 15 minutes

Cooking time: 55 minutes

Total time: 1 hour 10 minutes

Servings: 5

Ingredients:

- 2 tablespoons butter, divided
- 1/8 of yellow onion, chopped
- ¼ cup dried cranberries
- 2 cups celery stalks, chopped finely
- 1 apple, peeled, cored and chopped
- 1 teaspoon salt
- 5 (1-inch thick) boneless pork chops

How to Prepare:

1. Preheat your oven to 350°F.
2. In a Dutch oven, melt 1 tablespoon of butter over medium heat and sauté onion for about 4-6 minutes.
3. Remove from heat and immediately stir in cranberries, celery, apple, and salt.
4. Transfer the mixture into a bowl.
5. Place pork chops onto a cutting board.
6. With a sharp knife, cut one side, leaving the three sides intact.
7. Fill the chop pocket with cranberry mixture.
8. Now melt remaining butter in the Dutch oven over medium heat.
9. Add chops and cook for about 2 minutes per side.
10. Cover the Dutch oven and transfer into the oven.
11. Bake for approximately 45 minutes.
12. Remove from oven and transfer the chops onto a plate.
13. Serve hot.

Nutritional Values:

Calories 318, Total Fat 10.7 g, Saturated Fat 5 g, Cholesterol 136 mg, Sodium 628mg, Total Carbs 8.1 g, Fiber 2 g, Sugar 5.5 g, Protein 45 g

Sausage & Bacon Bread Casserole

Preparation time: 29 minutes

Cooking time: 1 hour 10 minutes

Total time: 1½ hours

Servings: 8

Ingredients:

- 1 pound bacon slices
- 1 pound ground pork sausage
- 6 processed American cheese slices, shredded
- 3 small onions, chopped
- 12 white bread slices, crust removed
- 2 tablespoons butter, softened
- 8 eggs
- 4 cups milk

How to Prepare:

1. Lightly grease a 13x9-inch baking dish. Set aside.
2. Heat 2 non-stick woks over medium-high heat at the same time.
3. In a wok, add bacon and cook for about 8-10 minutes or until crispy. Transfer the bacon into a large bowl.
4. Meanwhile, in another wok, add sausage and cook for about 8-10 minutes.
5. Transfer the sausage into the bowl with bacon.
6. Crumble both bacon and sausage and let them cool.
7. In the bowl of bacon mixture, add cheese and onion and mix well.
8. Spread butter over 6 slices of bread evenly.
9. Arrange buttered slices in the bottom of the prepared baking dish, butter side up.
10. Spread half of bacon mixture over buttered slices evenly.
11. Arrange remaining slices over bacon mixture evenly.
12. Top with the remaining bacon mixture.
13. In a bowl, add eggs and milk and beat until well blended.
14. Pour milk mixture over bread slices evenly.
15. With a large piece of foil, cover the baking dish.
16. Refrigerate overnight.
17. Preheat your oven to 425°F.
18. Bake for approximately 40-60 minutes.
19. Serve hot.

Nutritional Values:

Calories 799, Total Fat 54.6 g, Saturated Fat 20 g, Cholesterol 304 mg, Sodium 1537 mg, Total Carbs 28.5 g, Fiber 1.7 g, Sugar 9.2 g, Protein 48.1 g

Braised Lamb Shanks

Preparation time: 15 minutes

Cooking time: 3 hours 10 minutes

Total time: 3 hours 25 minutes

Servings: 6

Ingredients:

- 6 lamb shanks
- Salt and ground black pepper, as required
- 2 tablespoons olive oil
- 3 large carrots, peeled and chopped
- 2 onions, chopped
- 10 garlic cloves, minced
- 1 (28-ounce) can peeled tomatoes with juices
- 1 bottle red wine
- 1 (10½-ounce) can condensed chicken broth
- 1 (10½-ounce) can beef broth
- 5 teaspoons fresh rosemary, chopped
- 2 teaspoons fresh thyme, chopped
- ¼ cup fresh parsley, chopped

How to Prepare:

1. Rub the shanks with salt and black pepper.
2. In a Dutch oven, heat the oil over medium-high heat and cook the shanks in 2 batches for about 8 minutes.
3. With a slotted spoon, transfer the cooked shanks onto a plate.
4. In the same pan, add the carrots, onions, and garlic and cook for about 10 minutes, stirring frequently.
5. Add the tomatoes, wine, chicken broth, beef broth, rosemary, and thyme and stir to combine.
6. Add the cooked shanks and press down to submerge in the broth mixture.
7. Now adjust the heat to high and bring to a boil.
8. Now adjust the heat to medium-low and simmer, covered for about 2 hours.
9. Uncover and simmer for about 20 minutes.
10. With tongs, transfer the shanks onto a platter and with a piece of foil, cover them to keep warm.
11. Place the pan of cooking juices over medium heat and cook for about 15-20 minutes or until desired thickness.
12. Place the pan juices over shanks and serve with the garnishing of parsley.

Nutritional Values:

Calories 991, Total 57.7 g, Saturated Fat 25 g, Cholesterol 301 mg, Sodium 507 mg, Total Carbs 16.2 g, Fiber 4 g, Sugar 7.3 g, Protein 90.1 g

Pan-Seared Lamb Chops

Preparation time: 10 minutes

Cooking time: 6 minutes

Total time: 16 minutes

Servings: 4

Ingredients:

- 4 garlic cloves, peeled
- Salt, as required
- 1 teaspoon black mustard seeds, crushed finely
- 2 teaspoons ground cumin
- 1 teaspoon ground ginger
- 1 teaspoon ground coriander
- ½ teaspoon ground cinnamon
- Ground black pepper, as required
- 1 tablespoon coconut oil
- 8 medium lamb chops, trimmed

How to Prepare:

1. Place the garlic cloves onto a cutting board and sprinkle with some salt.
2. With a knife, crush the garlic until a paste forms.
3. In a bowl, blend together garlic paste and spices.
4. With a sharp knife, make 3-4 cuts on both sides of the chops.
5. Rub the chops with garlic mixture generously.
6. In a large-sized cast-iron wok, melt the coconut oil over medium heat and cook the chops for about 3 minutes per side.
7. Serve hot.

Nutritional Values:

Calories 437, Total Fat 17.1 g, Saturated Fat 6 g, Cholesterol 204 mg, Sodium 214 mg, Total Carbs 2.3 g, Fiber 0.5 g, Sugar 0.1 g, Protein 64.3 g

Pork with Brussels Sprouts

Preparation time: 15 minutes

Cooking time: 10 minutes

Total time: 25 minutes

Servings: 4

Ingredients:

- 3 tablespoons butter
- 1 1/3 pounds pork belly, cut into bite-sized pieces
- 1 pound Brussels sprouts, trimmed and halved
- 2 garlic cloves, minced
- 2 tablespoons low-sodium soy sauce
- 1 tablespoon balsamic vinegar
- Ground black pepper, as required
- 1 scallion, sliced

How to Prepare:

1. In a large-sized wok, melt the butter over medium-high heat and cook the pork pieces for about 3-4 minutes or until golden brown.
2. Stir in the Brussels sprouts and garlic and stir fry for about 3-4 minutes.
3. Add the soy sauce, vinegar, and black pepper and cook for about 1-2 minutes.
4. Stir in the scallion and serve hot.

Nutritional Values:

Calories 447, Total Fat 37.1 g, Saturated Fat 14.4 g, Cholesterol 82 mg, Sodium 837 mg, Total Carbs 9.3 g, Fiber 3.5 g, Sugar 2.5 g, Protein 22.2 g

FISH & SEAFOOD

Fish and seafood carry many great vitamins and nutrients that will help keep you healthy and warm during the winter months. Keep your family or friends warm with these delightful dishes.

Stuffed Salmon 90
Salmon Pie 92
Scalloped Oysters 94
Tuna Casserole 96
Shrimp & Tomato Bake 98
Seafood Casserole 100
Tilapia & Tomato Casserole 102
Creamy Salmon Casserole 103
Seared Tuna 104
Bacon-Wrapped Salmon 105

Stuffed Salmon

Preparation time: 15 minutes

Cooking time: 16 minutes

Total time: 31 minutes

Servings: 4

Ingredients:

Salmon

- 4 (6-ounce) skinless salmon fillets
- Salt and ground black pepper, as required
- 2 tablespoons fresh lemon juice
- 2 tablespoons olive oil, divided
- 1 tablespoon unsalted butter

Filling

- 4 ounces cream cheese, softened
- ¼ cup parmesan cheese, grated finely
- 4 ounces frozen spinach, thawed and squeezed
- 2 teaspoons garlic, minced
- Salt and ground black pepper, as required

How to Prepare:

1. Rub the salmon fillets with salt and black pepper evenly and then drizzle each with lemon juice and 1 tablespoon of oil.
2. Place the salmon fillets onto a large-sized cutting board.
3. Carefully cut a pocket into each salmon fillet about ¾ of the way through (be careful not to cut all the way).
4. For filling: in a medium-sized bowl, blend together cream cheese, parmesan cheese, spinach, garlic, salt, and black pepper.
5. Place about 1-2 tablespoons of filling mixture into each salmon pocket and spread evenly.
6. In a wok, heat the remaining oil with butter over medium-high heat.
7. Place the salmon fillets into the wok and cook for about 6-8 minutes per side.
8. Remove the wok of salmon fillets from the heat and transfer onto the serving plates.
9. Serve immediately.

Nutritional Values:

Calories 438, Total Fat 31.7g, Saturated Fat 11.2 g, Cholesterol 118 mg, Sodium 285 mg, Total Carbs 2.4 g, Fiber 0.7 g, Sugar 0.4 g, Protein 38.1 g

Salmon Pie

Preparation time: 20 minutes

Cooking time: 50 minutes

Total time: 1 hour 10 minutes

Servings: 5

Ingredients:

Crust

- ¾ cup almond flour
- 4 tablespoons coconut flour
- 4 tablespoons sesame seeds
- 1 tablespoon psyllium husk powder
- 1 teaspoon baking powder
- Pinch of salt
- 1 egg
- 3 tablespoons olive oil
- 4 tablespoons water

Filling

- 8 ounces smoked salmon, chopped
- 4¼ ounces cream cheese, softened
- 1¼ cups cheddar cheese, shredded
- 1 cup mayonnaise
- 3 eggs
- 2 tablespoons fresh dill, finely chopped
- ½ teaspoon onion powder
- ¼ teaspoon ground black pepper

How to Prepare:

1. Preheat your oven to 350°F.
2. Line a 10-inch spring form pan with lightly greased baking paper.
3. For crust: place all the ingredients in a food processor fitted with a plastic pastry blade and pulse until a dough comes together.
4. In the bottom of greased pan, place the dough and with your fingers, gently press into the bottom.
5. Bake for approximately 13-15 minutes or until lightly browned.
6. Remove the pie crust from oven and let it cool slightly.
7. Meanwhile, for filling: in a bowl, add all the ingredients and mix well.
8. Place the mixture over the pie crust evenly.
9. Bake for approximately 34-35 minutes or until the pie is golden brown.
10. Remove the pie from oven and let it cool slightly.
11. Cut into 5 equal-sized slices and serve warm.

Nutritional Values:

Calories 734, Total Fat 59.5 g, Saturated Fat 17.8 g, Cholesterol 210 mg, Sodium 1037 mg, Total Carbs 24.8 g, Fiber 6.7 g, Sugar 3.6 g, Protein 28 g

Scalloped Oysters

Preparation time: 15 minutes

Cooking time: 1 hour

Total time: 1¼ hours

Servings: 8

Ingredients:

- 4 tablespoons unsalted butter
- 2 leeks, thinly sliced
- 1 tablespoon all-purpose flour
- ½ cup dry vermouth
- ½ cup heavy cream
- 1 cup Saltines, crushed
- 2 (16-ounce) containers fresh oysters, drained, reserving 2 tablespoons brine

How to Prepare:

1. Preheat your oven to 350°F.
2. Melt butter in a large-sized sauté pan over medium heat and cook leeks for about 6-7 minutes, stirring occasionally.
3. Slowly add in the flour and cook for 1 minute, stirring continuously.
4. Add vermouth and cook for about 2-3 minutes, stirring continuously.
5. Stir in the cream and again bring to a gentle simmer.
6. Remove from the heat and fold in oysters and brine.
7. Transfer the mixture into an 11x7-inch baking dish and evenly top with Saltines.
8. Bake for approximately 40-45 minutes or until golden brown.
9. Remove the baking dish of scalloped oysters from oven and set aside for about 5 minutes before serving.

Nutritional Values:

Calories 265, Total Fat1 4 g, Saturated Fat 6.8 g, Cholesterol 181 mg, Sodium 366 mg, Total Carbs 13.9 g, Fiber 0.6 g, Sugar 1 g, Protein 4.17 g

Tuna Casserole

Preparation time: 15 minutes

Cooking time: 25 minutes

Total time: 40 minutes

Servings: 4

Ingredients:

- 2 ounces butter
- 5 1/3 ounces celery stalks, chopped
- 1 yellow onion, chopped
- 1 bell pepper, seeded and chopped
- Salt and ground black pepper, as required
- 16 ounces canned tuna in olive oil, drained
- 4 ounces parmesan cheese, shredded
- 1 cup mayonnaise
- 1 teaspoon chili flakes

How to Prepare:

1. Preheat your oven to 400°F.
2. Grease a large baking dish.
3. In a large-sized sauté pan, melt the butter over medium heat and sauté the celery, onion, and bell pepper for about 4-5 minutes.
4. Add the salt and black pepper and stir to combine.
5. Remove the sauté pan from heat.
6. Place the tuna, parmesan cheese, mayonnaise, and chili flakes into the prepared baking dish and mix well.
7. Add the onion mixture and gently stir to combine.
8. Bake for approximately 15-20 minutes or until the top becomes golden brown.
9. Remove the baking dish from oven and let it cool for about 5 minutes before serving.

Nutritional Values:

Calories 659, Total Fat 47.1 g, Saturated Fat 15.9 g, Cholesterol 98 mg, Sodium 997 mg, Total Carbs 21 g, Fiber 1.6 g, Sugar 7 g, Protein 41.4 g

Shrimp & Tomato Bake

Preparation time: 15 minutes

Cooking time: 30 minutes

Total time: 45 minutes

Servings: 6

Ingredients:

- ¼ cup butter
- 1 tablespoon garlic, minced
- ¾ teaspoon dried oregano, crushed
- ¼ teaspoon red pepper flakes, crushed
- ¼ cup fresh parsley, chopped
- ¾ cup dry vermouth
- 1 (14½-ounce) can diced tomatoes
- 4 ounces feta cheese, crumbled
- 1½ pounds large shrimp, peeled and deveined

How to Prepare:

1. Preheat your oven to 350°F.
2. In a large-sized sauté pan, melt butter over medium-high heat and sauté the garlic for about 1 minute.
3. Add the shrimp, oregano, and red pepper flakes and cook for about 4-5 minutes.
4. Stir in the parsley and salt and immediately transfer into a casserole dish evenly.
5. In the same sauté pan, add vermouth on medium heat. Simmer for about 2-3 minutes or until it is reduced to half.
6. Stir in tomatoes and cook for about 2-3 minutes.
7. Place the tomato mixture over shrimp mixture evenly.
8. Top with cheese evenly.
9. Bake for approximately 16-20 minutes.
10. Serve hot.

Nutritional Values:

Calories 250, Total Fat 11.9 g, Saturated Fat 7.7 g, Cholesterol 199 mg, Sodium 414mg, Total Carbs 7.1 g, Fiber 1 g, Sugar 2.9 g, Protein 248 g

Seafood Casserole

Preparation time: 25 minutes

Cooking time: 1 hour 5 minutes

Total time: 1½ hours

Servings: 8

Ingredients:

- 2½ cups water
- 1 cup celery, chopped
- 1 medium yellow onion, chopped
- 3 tablespoons unsalted butter
- 1 cup heavy cream
- 1½ cups cheddar cheese, shredded and divided.
- Salt and ground black pepper, as required
- ½ pound fresh scallops, side muscles removed
- ½ pound shrimp, peeled and deveined
- 1½ cups lobster meat, chopped
- 1½ cups crab meat, chopped

How to Prepare:

1. Preheat your oven to 325°F.
2. In a large-sized saucepan, place the water over medium-high heat and bring to a boil.
3. Add onion and celery and boil for about 6 minutes.
4. With a slotted spoon, place the cooked vegetables into a large bowl.
5. In the same boiling water, add the scallops over low heat and cook for about 3 minutes.
6. With a slotted spoon, transfer scallops into the bowl of vegetables.
7. Again, in the same pan of boiling water, add the shrimp over low heat and cook for about 4 minutes.
8. With a slotted spoon, transfer shrimp into the bowl of vegetables.
9. In another small bowl, reserve ¾ cup of cooking water and set aside.
10. In the bowl of shrimp mixture, add the lobster and crab meat and mix well.
11. In a large wok, place the butter over medium heat and cook until it starts to brown.
12. Slowly add the cream and reserved cooking water, beating continuously until well blended.
13. Cook for about 1-2 minutes or until the sauce thickens slightly.
14. In the sauce, add 1 cup of cheese and stir until melted completely.
15. Stir in the seafood mixture, salt and black pepper and remove from the heat.
16. Place the mixture into a 9x13-inch baking dish evenly and top with the remaining cheddar cheese.
17. Bake for approximately 35-45 minutes.
18. Remove the baking dish from oven and let it cool for about 5 minutes before serving.

Nutritional Values:

Calories 271, Total Fat 17.9 g, Saturated Fat 10.9 g, Cholesterol 166 mg, Sodium 487 mg, Total Carbs 3.5 g, Fiber 0.5 g, Sugar 0.9 g, Protein 22.9 g

Tilapia & Tomato Casserole

Preparation time: 15 minutes

Cooking time: 14 minutes

Total time: 29 minutes

Servings: 4

Ingredients:

- 2 (14-ounce) cans diced tomatoes with basil and garlic with juice
- 1/3 cup fresh parsley, chopped and divided
- ¼ teaspoon dried oregano
- ½ teaspoon red pepper flakes, crushed
- 2 tablespoons fresh lemon juice
- 2/3 cup feta cheese, crumbled
- 4 (6-ounce) tilapia fillets

How to Prepare:

1. Preheat your oven to 400°F.
2. In a baking dish, add the tomatoes, ¼ cup of the parsley, oregano, and red pepper flakes and mix until well blended.
3. Arrange the tilapia fillets over the tomato mixture in a single layer and drizzle with the lemon juice.
4. Place some tomato mixture over the tilapia fillets and sprinkle with the feta cheese evenly.
5. Bake for approximately 12-14 minutes.
6. Serve hot with the garnishing of remaining parsley.

Nutritional Values:

Calories 246, Total Fat 7.4 g, Saturated Fat 4.6 g, Cholesterol 105 mg, Sodium 353 mg, Total Carbs 9.4 g, Fiber 2.7 g, Sugar 6.5 g, Protein 37.2 g

Creamy Salmon Casserole

Preparation time: 10 minutes

Cooking time: 20 minutes

Total time: 30 minutes

Servings: 2

Ingredients:

- ¼ cup
- cream cheese, softened
- 2 tablespoons fresh chives, chopped
- 1 teaspoon garlic powder
- ¼ teaspoon cayenne pepper
- Salt and ground black pepper, as required
- 2 (4-ounce) salmon fillets

How to Prepare:

1. Preheat your oven to 350°F.
2. Lightly grease a small baking dish.
3. In a bowl, add the cream cheese, chives, spices, salt, and black pepper and mix well.
4. Arrange the salmon fillets into the prepared baking dish and top with the cream cheese mixture evenly.
5. Bake for approximately 16-20 minutes or until desired doneness of the salmon.
6. Serve hot.

Nutritional Values:

Calories 257, Total Fat 17.2 g, Saturated Fat 7.4 g, Cholesterol 82 mg, Sodium 214 mg, Total Carbs 2.1 g, Fiber 0.3 g, Sugar 0.5 g, Protein 34.6 g

Seared Tuna

Preparation time: 10 minutes

Cooking time: 2 minutes

Total time: 12 minutes

Servings: 2

Ingredients:

- 2 (4-ounce) ahi tuna steaks
- Salt and ground black pepper, as required
- vegetable oil
- 4 tablespoons sesame seeds
- 1 tablespoon

How to Prepare:

1. Rub the tuna steaks with salt and black pepper evenly.
2. Place the sesame seeds onto a shallow plate.
3. Gently press tuna steaks into seeds to coat evenly.
4. In a medium wok, heat oil over medium-high heat and sear the tuna for about 1 minute per side or until desired doneness.
5. Transfer the tuna steaks onto a cutting board.
6. Cut each tuna steak into desired-sized slices and serve.

Nutritional Values:

Calories 372, Total Fat 22.9 g, Saturated Fat 4.4 g, Cholesterol 56 mg, Sodium 137 mg, Total Carbs 4.2 g, Fiber 2.1 g, Sugar 0.1 g, Protein 37.1 g

Bacon-Wrapped Salmon

Preparation time: 10 minutes

Cooking time: 15 minutes

Total time: 25 minutes

Servings: 2

Ingredients:

- 2 (6-ounce) salmon fillets
- 2 streaky bacon slices

How to Prepare:

1. Preheat your oven to 350°F.
2. Line a medium-sized baking sheet with lightly greased baking paper.
3. Wrap each salmon fillet with 1 bacon slice and then secure with a wooden skewer.
4. Arrange the wrapped salmon fillets onto the prepared baking sheet.
5. Bake for approximately 15 minutes.
6. Serve hot.

Nutritional Values:

Calories 382, Total Fat 22.6 g, Saturated Fat 5.5 g, Cholesterol 107 mg, Sodium 745 mg, Total Carbs 0.4 g, Fiber 0 g, Sugar 0 g, Protein 43.7 g

WARM SOUPS & STEWS

Nothing keeps you warm during the long winter months like a delicious soup or hearty stew. Make these meals and freeze them to have at any time, especially when you need a quick bowl of delightful warmth.

Lentil & Sweet Potato Soup 107
Turkey & Wild Rice Soup 108
Bacon & Tortellini Soup 110
French Onion Soup 112
Creamy Pumpkin Soup 114
Chicken & Mushroom Stew 116
Turkey & Pasta Stew 118
Beef Stew in a Pumpkin 120
Pork Stew 122
Potato & Bean Stew 124

Lentil & Sweet Potato Soup

Preparation time: 15 minutes

Cooking time: 40 minutes

Total time: 55 minutes

Servings: 6

Ingredients:

- 1 tablespoon vegetable oil
- 4 leeks, chopped
- 1¾ cups tomatoes, chopped
- 6 cups vegetable broth
- ½ cup brown lentils, rinsed
- 2 sweet potatoes, peeled and cubed
- 4 cups fresh kale, tough ribs removed and chopped
- 1 tablespoon fresh thyme, chopped
- Salt and ground black pepper, as required

How to Prepare:

1. In a large-sized soup pan, heat oil over medium heat and sauté leeks for about 3-4 minutes.
2. Add tomatoes and cook for 5-6 minutes, crushing with the back of a spoon.
3. Add broth and bring to a boil.
4. Add lentils, sweet potato, kale, and thyme and again bring to a boil.
5. Now adjust the heat to low and simmer, covered for about 25-30 minutes or until desired doneness.
6. Stir in salt and black pepper and serve hot.

Nutritional Values:

Calories 239, Total Fat 4.2 g, Saturated Fat 0.9 g, Cholesterol 0 mg, Sodium 830 mg, Total Carbs 38.9 g, Fiber 9.3 g, Sugar 5 g, Protein 12.4 g

Turkey & Wild Rice Soup

Preparation time: 20 minutes

Cooking time: 2 hours 5 minutes

Total time: 2 hours 25 minutes

Servings: 6

Ingredients:

- 2 smoked turkey legs
- 1 cup baby carrots, sliced
- 1 onion, chopped
- 2 cups celery stalks, chopped
- 2 garlic cloves, minced
- 2 bay leaves
- 1 teaspoon dried marjoram, crushed
- 1 teaspoon dried thyme, crushed
- 1 tablespoon onion powder
- 1 tablespoon garlic powder
- 2 teaspoons ground black pepper
- 1 teaspoon curry powder
- 4 chicken bouillon cubes
- 8 cups water
- 1 cup uncooked wild rice
- 4 cups half-and-half

How to Prepare:

1. In a large soup pan, add all ingredients except rice and half-and-half over high heat and bring to a boil.
2. Now adjust the heat to low and simmer for about 30 minutes.
3. Stir in rice and simmer for about 1 hour.
4. Transfer the turkey legs into a large bowl and let them cool.
5. Pull the meat from bones and then chop it.
6. Stir in half-and-half and turkey meat and simmer for about 30 minutes.

Nutritional Values:

Calories 498, Total Fat 24.3 g, Saturated Fat 13.3 g, Cholesterol 126 mg, Sodium 602 mg, Total Carbs 33.4 g, Fiber 3.3 g, Sugar 3.5 g, Protein 37 g

Bacon & Tortellini Soup

Preparation time: 15 minutes

Cooking time: 30 minutes

Total time: 45 minutes

Servings: 8

Ingredients:

- 2 tablespoons olive oil
- 2 ounces bacon, chopped finely
- 1 medium onion, chopped finely
- 3 garlic cloves, minced
- 1 (49½-ounce) can chicken broth
- 2 teaspoons Italian seasoning
- 1 (9-ounce) package refrigerated cheese tortellini
- 1 (28-ounce) can crushed tomatoes with juices
- 8 ounces fresh spinach, chopped
- Salt and ground black pepper, as required
- 1 cup Parmesan cheese, shredded

How to Prepare:

1. Heat the oil in a large-sized Dutch oven over medium heat and cook the bacon for about 8-10 minutes or until crisp.
2. Add the onion and cook for about 3-4 minutes, stirring continuously.
3. Add garlic and cook for about 1 minute, stirring continuously.
4. Add broth and Italian seasoning and bring to a boil.
5. Cook for about 5 minutes.
6. Meanwhile, cook tortellini according to package's directions.
7. Drain the tortellini.
8. Add the cooked tortellini and tomatoes into soup mixture and cook for about 5 minutes.
9. Add spinach and cook for about 3-5 minutes.
10. Season with salt and black pepper and serve hot with the garnishing of Parmesan cheese.

Nutritional Values:

Calories 294, Total Fat 12.6 g, Saturated 3.6 g, Cholesterol 22 mg, Sodium 837 mg, Total Carbs 524.8 g, Fiber 4.1 g, Sugar 6.9 g , Protein 17.2g

French Onion Soup

Preparation time: 15 minutes

Cooking time: 50 minutes

Total time: 1 hour 5 minutes

Servings: 4

Ingredients:

- 4 tablespoons butter
- 3 large white onions, thinly sliced
- 2 tablespoons all-purpose flour
- ½ cup white wine
- Salt and ground black pepper, as required
- 8 fresh thyme sprigs
- 2 cups low-sodium chicken broth
- 4 cups low-sodium beef broth
- 4 baguette slices
- ½ cup Gruyere cheese, grated

How to Prepare:

1. Melt butter in a large-sized soup pan over medium-high heat and cook onions for about 25 minutes, stirring occasionally.
2. Add flour and immediately stir to combine.
3. Cook for about 1 minute, stirring continuously.
4. Stir in wine, salt, and black pepper and simmer for about 2-3 minutes.
5. Add thyme sprigs, chicken, and beef broths and bring to a boil.
6. Now adjust the heat to medium and simmer for about 15 minutes.
7. Preheat the broiler of the oven to high.
8. Remove the soup pan from heat and discard the thyme sprigs.
9. Place baguette slices on a large-sized baking sheet and top each slice with 2 tablespoons of cheese.
10. Transfer the baking sheet into oven and broil for about 1 minute or until cheese is bubbling and golden brown.
11. Transfer soup into bowls and serve with the topping of slices.

Nutritional Values:

Calories 319, Total Fat 19 g, Saturated Fat 9.9 g, Cholesterol 45 mg, Sodium 432 mg, Total Carbs 21.5 g, Fiber 2.7 g, Sugar 5.1 g, Protein 10.1 g

Creamy Pumpkin Soup

Preparation time: 15 minutes

Cooking time: 50 minutes

Total time: 1 hour 5 minutes

Servings: 4

Ingredients:

- 2 small sugar pumpkins, halved and seeded
- 3 cups chicken broth
- ¾ cup heavy whipping cream
- ¼ cup sour cream
- ½ teaspoon ground sage, crushed
- ¼ teaspoon ground nutmeg
- 1½ teaspoons salt

How to Prepare:

1. Preheat your oven to 400°F.
2. Grease a baking sheet.
3. Place pumpkins onto the prepared baking sheet, cut side down.
4. Roast for approximately 45 minutes.
5. Remove the pumpkins from the oven and let them cool completely.
6. After cooling, scrape out the flesh of the pumpkins.
7. In a food processor, add pumpkin flesh and broth and pulse until smooth.
8. Transfer the pureed soup into a large-sized saucepan.
9. Place the pan over medium heat and bring to a gentle simmer.
10. Then, stir in whipping cream, sage, nutmeg, and salt until well blended.
11. Transfer the soup into serving bowls.
12. Top with sour cream and serve hot.

Nutritional Values:

Calories 215, Total Fat 13.1 g, Saturated Fat 7.7 g, Cholesterol 37 mg, Sodium 837 mg, Total Carbs 20.4 g, Fiber 6.6 g, Sugar 8.1 g, Protein 7.1 g

Chicken & Mushroom Stew

Preparation time: 15 minutes

Cooking time: 35 minutes

Total time: 50 minutes

Servings: 6

Ingredients:

- 3 tablespoons unsalted butter
- ½ cup yellow onion, chopped
- ¾ cup bell pepper, seeded and chopped
- 3¾ cups chicken broth
- 1 bay leaf
- 2 tablespoons fresh thyme, minced
- Salt and ground black pepper, as required
- 2/3 cup whipping cream
- 15 ounces fresh asparagus, ends trimmed and cut into medium-sized pieces
- 8 ounces fresh mushrooms, sliced
- 1¼ cup fresh green beans, ends trimmed
- 2½ pounds cooked boneless chicken, chopped

How to Prepare:

1. In a large-sized, heavy-bottomed soup pan, melt the butter over medium heat and sauté the onion and bell pepper for about 4-5 minutes.
2. Add in the broth and bay leaf and bring to a boil.
3. Cook for about 10 minutes.
4. Meanwhile, in a small-sized pan, add cream over medium heat and cook for about 5-7 minutes, stirring occasionally.
5. Add the asparagus, mushrooms, and green beans into the pan of broth mixture and cook for about 7-10 minutes.
6. In the stew, add the cooked chicken and stir to combine.
7. Now adjust the heat to low and simmer for about 3-5 minutes.
8. Stir in the salt, black pepper, and thyme and immediately remove from the heat.
9. Serve hot.

Nutritional Values:

Calories 464, Total Fat 17.8 g, Saturated Fat 8.4 g, Cholesterol 176 mg, Sodium 537 mg, Total Carbs 9 g, Fiber 2.9 g, Sugar 4.1 g, Protein 64.9 g

Turkey & Pasta Stew

Preparation time: 15 minutes

Cooking time: 40 minutes

Total time: 55 minutes

Servings: 8

Ingredients:

- 1½ pounds lean ground turkey
- 1 carrot, peeled and chopped
- 1 celery stalk, chopped
- 1 cup tomato sauce
- 1 (14-ounce) can stewed, diced tomatoes
- 2 teaspoons white sugar
- 3 garlic cloves, minced
- ½ teaspoon dried basil, crushed
- 1 (16-ounce) package dried pasta (of your choice)

How to Prepare:

1. Heat a large-sized non-stick soup pan over medium heat and cook turkey for about 8-10 minutes or until browned.
2. Stir in the carrot, celery, tomato sauce, tomatoes, sugar, garlic cloves, and basil and bring to a gentle boil.
3. Now adjust the heat to low and simmer for about 20 minutes.
4. Meanwhile, in a large-sized saucepan of salted boiling water, add pasta and cook for about 8-10 minutes.
5. Drain the pasta well.
6. Add pasta into the pan with turkey mixture and cook for about 4-5 minutes.
7. Serve hot.

Nutritional Values:

Calories 310, Total Fat 7.6 g, Saturated Fat 2.1 g, Cholesterol 102 mg, Sodium 249 mg, Total Carbs 36.8 g, Fiber 1.3 g, Sugar 4 g, Protein 21.4 g

Beef Stew in a Pumpkin

Preparation time: 20 minutes

Cooking time: 4 hours 10 minutes

Total time: 4½ hours

Servings: 8

Ingredients:

- 3 tablespoons extra-virgin olive oil, divided
- 1 onion, chopped
- 1 large bell pepper, seeded and chopped
- 4 cups carrots, peeled and chopped
- 1 (14½-ounce) can whole peeled tomatoes, chopped
- 1 sugar pumpkin, cut off the top, seeds and pulp removed
- 4 garlic cloves, minced
- 1 cup water
- Salt and ground black pepper, s required
- 2 tablespoons beef bouillon granules
- 2 pounds beef stew meat, cubed

How to Prepare:

1. In a large-sized soup pan, heat 2 tablespoons of oil over medium-high heat and sear beef for about 5 minutes.
2. Stir in vegetables, water, and seasoning and bring to a boil.
3. Now adjust the heat to low and simmer, covered for about 2 hours.
4. Preheat your oven to 325°F.
5. In the simmering stew, stir in beef bouillon granules and remove from heat.
6. Now, set the pumpkin in a baking dish.
7. Grease the outside of the pumpkin with remaining oil evenly.
8. Carefully transfer the stew into the hollowed pumpkin.
9. Bake for approximately 2 hours or until pumpkin becomes tender.
10. While serving, scrap some pumpkin meat from inside and serve with the stew.

Nutritional Values:

Calories 339, Total Fat 12.8 g, Saturated Fat 3.6 g, Cholesterol 101 mg, Sodium 164 mg, Total Carbs 19.5 g, Fiber 5.8 g, Sugar 9.2 g, Protein 3.7 g

Pork Stew

Preparation time: 20 minutes

Cooking time: 1 hour 25 minutes

Total time: 1¾ hours

Servings: 8

Ingredients:

- 2½ pounds boneless pork roast, trimmed and cubed
- ¼ cup all-purpose flour
- Salt and ground black pepper, as required
- 3 tablespoons extra-virgin olive oil
- 2 small leeks, thinly sliced
- 1 cup shallots, chopped
- 4 large garlic cloves, minced
- 1 cup white wine
- 4 medium potatoes, peeled and cubed
- 5 medium carrots, peeled and cut into ¾-inch pieces
- 1 (18-ounce) can diced tomatoes
- 2 cups chicken broth
- 2 tablespoons balsamic vinegar
- 2 bay leaves
- 1 teaspoon dried thyme
- 1 teaspoon dried oregano
- 1 teaspoon dried basil
- 10 ounces cremini mushrooms, cut in half
- ½ cup fresh parsley, chopped

How to Prepare:

1. In a medium bowl, add in pork cubes, flour, ½ teaspoon of salt, and ½ teaspoon of black pepper and toss to coat well.
2. Heat olive oil in a large-sized Dutch oven over medium-high heat and cook the pork cubes in 2 batches for about 2-3 minutes each.
3. Transfer the browned pork onto a plate.
4. In the same pan, add leeks, shallots, and garlic and sauté for about 2-3 minutes.
5. Add in the wine and scrape the browned bits from the bottom.
6. Add potatoes, carrots, tomatoes, broth, vinegar, bay leaves, thyme, oregano, basil, salt, and black pepper and bring to a boil.
7. Now adjust the heat to low and simmer for about 5 minutes.
8. Stir in the cooked pork and simmer, covered for about 45-50 minutes.
9. Add mushrooms and simmer for about 10-15 minutes.
10. Serve hot with the garnishing of parsley.

Nutritional Values:

Calories 430, Total Fat 11.1 g, Saturated Fat 2.6 g, Cholesterol 103 mg, Sodium 342 mg, Total Carbs 34.4 g, Fiber 3.9 g, Sugar 6.1 g, Protein 43.3 g

Potato & Bean Stew

Preparation time: 15 minutes

Cooking time: 50 minutes

Total time: 1 hour 5 minutes

Servings: 6

Ingredients:

- 2 tablespoons olive oil
- 1 large onion, chopped
- 2 teaspoons red chili powder
- 1 teaspoon ground cumin
- 2 garlic cloves, minced
- Salt, as required
- Ground black pepper, as required
- 1 large bell pepper, seeded and chopped
- 2 medium poblano peppers, seeded and chopped
- 1½ pounds Yukon Gold potatoes, scrubbed and cut into 1-inch chunks
- 1 cup water
- 30 ounces canned pinto beans, rinsed and drained
- 1 (15-ounce) can diced tomatoes with juices
- 2 tablespoons fresh lime juice

How to Prepare:

1. In a large-sized Dutch oven, heat the oil over medium heat and sauté the onion, chili powder, and cumin for about 5 minutes.
2. Add the bell pepper, poblano peppers, garlic, and salt and cook for about 5 minutes, stirring occasionally.
3. Add the potatoes and stir to combine.
4. Now adjust the heat to low and simmer, covered for about 5 minutes, stirring occasionally.
5. Add the water and simmer, covered for about 20-30 minutes.
6. In the pan of stew, add the beans and tomatoes with juices and gently stir to combine.
7. Now adjust the heat to medium-high and bring to a boil.
8. Now adjust the heat to medium-low and cook, uncovered for about 5 minutes.
9. Stir in the lime juice, salt, and black pepper and remove from the heat.
10. Serve hot.

Nutritional Values:

Calories 316, Total Fat 6.1 g, Saturated Fat 0.9 g, Cholesterol 0 mg, Sodium 386 mg, Total Carbs 53.8 g, Fiber 15.6 g, Sugar 5.5 g, Protein 15.3 g

VEGETARIAN & VEGAN SIDE DISHES

Everyone deserves to be warmed and delighted by wonderful fall and winter dishes. Here are some scrumptious recipes that don't require meat or animal byproducts.

Rosemary Mushrooms 127
Potato Mash 128
Roasted Tomatoes 129
Roasted Cauliflower 130
Glazed Carrots 132
Nutty Brussels Sprouts 134
Glazed Sweet Potatoes 136
Baked Beans 138
Buttered Rice 140
Buttered Quinoa 142

Rosemary Mushrooms

Preparation time: 10 minutes

Cooking time: 20 minutes

Total time: 30 minutes

Servings: 5

Ingredients:

- 1½ pounds fresh mushrooms, sliced
- Salt and ground black pepper, as required
- 1 teaspoon dried rosemary
- ¼ cup olive oil

How to Prepare:

1. Preheat your oven to 400°F.
2. In a baking dish, place all the ingredients and toss to coat well.
3. Then, spread the mushrooms in an even layer.
4. Bake for approximately 20 minutes.
5. Serve hot.

Nutritional Values:

Calories 116, Total Fat 10.5 g, Saturated Fat 1.5 g, Cholesterol 0 mg, Sodium 37 mg, Total Carbs 4.6 g, Fiber 1.5 g, Sugar 2.3 g, Protein 4.3 g

Potato Mash

Preparation time: 15 minutes

Cooking time: 15 minutes

Total time: 30 minutes

Servings: 4

Ingredients:

- 2 pounds baking potatoes, peeled and quartered
- 2 tablespoons butter
- 1 cup milk
- Salt and ground black pepper, as required

How to Prepare:

1. In a large-sized saucepan of salted boiling water, cook the potatoes for about 15 minutes.
2. Drain the potatoes well.
3. In a small-sized pan, add milk and butter over low heat and cook for about 2-3 minutes, stirring regularly.
4. In a bowl, add cooked potatoes and with a potato masher, mash well.
5. Add milk mixture to the mash and mix until smooth and creamy.
6. Season with salt and pepper and serve.

Nutritional Values:

Calories 146, Total Fat 7.1g, Saturated Fat 4.4 g, Cholesterol 20 mg,

Sodium 117 mg, Total Carbs 18.2 g, Fiber 1.2 g, Sugar 3.3 g, Protein 3.8 g

Roasted Tomatoes

Preparation time: 15 minutes

Cooking time: 20 minutes

Total time: 35 minutes

Servings: 3

Ingredients:

- 6 large Roma tomatoes, halved
- Salt, as required
- 2 tablespoons olive oil

How to Prepare:

1. Sprinkle each tomato halves with the salt evenly.
2. Arrange the tomatoes onto a large paper towel-lined plate, cut side down.
3. Set aside for about 40 minutes to drain completely.
4. Preheat your oven to 425°F.
5. Grease a large-sized baking sheet.
6. In the bottom of the prepared baking sheet, arrange the tomato halves in a single layer, cut side up and then, drizzle with the oil.
7. Roast for approximately 20 minutes.
8. Remove the baking sheet of tomatoes from oven and set aside to cool slightly.
9. Serve warm.

Nutritional Values:

Calories 146, Total Fat 10.1 g, Saturated Fat 1.4 g, Cholesterol 0 mg, Sodium 68 mg, Total Carbs 14.2 g, Fiber 4.4 g, Sugar 9.5 g, Protein 3.2 g

Roasted Cauliflower

Preparation time: 15 minutes

Cooking time: 20 minutes

Total time: 35 minutes

Servings: 5

Ingredients:

- 4 cups cauliflower florets
- 4 small garlic cloves, peeled and halved
- 2 tablespoons olive oil
- 1 tablespoon fresh lemon juice
- 1 teaspoon dried thyme, crushed
- 1 teaspoon dried oregano, crushed
- ½ teaspoon cayenne pepper
- Salt and ground black pepper, as required

How to Prepare:

1. Preheat your oven to 425°F.

2. Generously grease 2 large baking dishes.

3. In a large-sized bowl, add cauliflower florets and remaining ingredients and toss to coat well.

4. Divide the cauliflower mixture into the prepared baking dishes evenly and spread in a single layer.

5. Roast for approximately 16-20 minutes or until the desired doneness, tossing 2 times.

6. Remove from the oven and serve hot.

Nutritional Values:

Calories 74, Total Fat 5.8 g, Saturated Fat 0.9 g, Cholesterol 0 mg, Sodium 25 mg, Total Carbs 5.4 g, Fiber 2.3 g, Sugar 2 g, Protein 1.8 g

Glazed Carrots

Preparation time: 15 minutes

Cooking time: 1 hour 10 minutes

Total time: 1 hour 25 minutes

Servings: 8

Ingredients:

- ½ cup butter
- 2 pounds carrots, peeled and sliced
- 1 cup honey
- 1 tablespoon fresh thyme, chopped
- Salt and ground black pepper, as required
- ¼ cup brown sugar

How to Prepare:

1. Preheat your oven to 350°F.
2. In a Dutch oven, add the butter and place in the oven until butter is melted.
3. Remove the Dutch oven and stir in the carrots.
4. Add the honey, thyme, salt, and black pepper and stir to combine.
5. Sprinkle the carrots with brown sugar evenly and bake for approximately 55-60 minutes or until the carrots are tender.
6. Remove the Dutch oven and with a slotted spoon, transfer the carrots onto a platter.
7. With a piece of foil, cover the carrots to keep warm.
8. Place the pan with any remaining honey sauce over medium-high heat and bring to a boil.
9. Cook for about 5 minutes, stirring occasionally.
10. Remove the pan of honey sauce from heat and pour over the carrots and stir to combine.
11. Serve immediately.

Nutritional Values:

Calories 295, Total Fat 11.5 g, Saturated Fat 7.3 g, Cholesterol 31 mg, Sodium 181 mg, Total Carbs 50.9g, Fiber 3 g, Sugar 44.8 g, Protein 1.2 g

Nutty Brussels Sprouts

Preparation time: 15 minutes

Cooking time: 25 minutes

Total time: 40 minutes

Servings: 6

Ingredients:

- 2 pounds Brussels sprouts, ends trimmed and yellow leaves removed
- ½ cup butter, cut into pieces
- Salt and ground black pepper, as required
- ¼ cup fresh lemon juice
- ¼ cup pine nuts

How to Prepare:

1. Preheat your oven to 350°F.
2. In a Dutch oven, place the Brussels sprouts and top with the butter pieces, followed by the salt, black pepper and lemon juice.
3. Cover the Dutch oven with a lid tightly and bake for approximately 15 minutes, stirring occasionally.
4. Remove the pan of Brussels sprouts from oven and sprinkle with the pine nuts.
5. Bake, uncovered for about 10 minutes, stirring twice.
6. Serve hot.

Nutritional Values:

Calories 242, Total Fat 19.8 g, Saturated Fat 10.7 g, Cholesterol 41 mg, Sodium 170 mg, Total Carbs 14.8 g, Fiber 5.9 g, Sugar 3.7 g, Protein 6.2 g

Glazed Sweet Potatoes

Preparation time: 15 minutes

Cooking time: 30 minutes

Total time: 45 minutes

Servings: 5

Ingredients:

- 1½ pounds medium-sized sweet potatoes, peeled and cut into 1-inch-thick slices
- ½ cup brown sugar
- 1/3 cup water
- 1 tablespoon butter
- Salt, as required

How to Prepare:

1. In a large Dutch oven, add the sweet potatoes and enough water to cover them and bring to a boil.
2. Cook for about 12-15 minutes or until just tender.
3. Remove from the heat and drain the sweet potatoes completely.
4. In the same pan, add the remaining ingredients over low heat and simmer for about 5 minutes, stirring frequently.
5. Stir in the sweet potato slices and simmer for about 10 minutes, stirring frequently.
6. Serve hot.

Nutritional Values:

Calories 236, Total Fat 2.5 g, Saturated Fat 1.5 g, Cholesterol 6 mg, Sodium 67 mg, Total Carbs 51.2 g, Fiber 5.6 g, Sugar 14.8 g, Protein 2.1 g

Baked Beans

Preparation time: 15 minutes

Cooking time: 50 minutes

Total time: 1 hour 5 minutes

Servings: 4

Ingredients:

- 1 tablespoon olive oil
- ½ cup green bell pepper, seeded and chopped
- ½ cup white onion, chopped
- 3 garlic cloves, minced
- Salt, as required
- Ground black pepper, as required
- 1¼ cups tomato sauce
- 5 tablespoons pure maple syrup
- ¼ cup water
- 1 tablespoon liquid smoke
- ¼ cup Worcestershire sauce
- 2 (14-ounces) cans Great Northern beans, drained and rinsed

How to Prepare:

1. Preheat your oven to 325°F.
2. In a large-sized cast-iron wok, heat the oil over medium heat and cook the bell pepper, onion, garlic, and salt for about 4-5 minutes.
3. Add the remaining ingredients except for the beans and stir to combine.
4. Add the beans and gently stir to combine.
5. Transfer the wok into the oven and bake for approximately 30-45 minutes.
6. Serve hot.

Nutritional Values:

Calories 377, Total Fat 4.5 g, Saturated Fat 0.8 g, Cholesterol 0 mg, Sodium 515 mg, Total Carbs 69 g, Fiber 15.6 g, Sugar 22.5 g, Protein 18 g

Buttered Rice

Preparation time: 10 minutes

Cooking time: 25 minutes

Total time: 35 minutes

Servings: 5

Ingredients:

- 1½ cups rice, rinsed
- 2 tablespoons butter
- 1 small onion, chopped
- 2¾ cups chicken broth
- Salt, as required

How to Prepare:

1. Preheat your oven to 350°F.
2. In a small-sized Dutch oven, melt the butter and cook the onion for about 5 minutes, stirring frequently.
3. Add the rice and cook for about 2 minutes, stirring frequently.
4. Add the broth and salt and bring to a boil.
5. Immediately cover the pan with a lid tightly and transfer into the oven.
6. Bake for approximately 15 minutes.
7. Remove from the oven and set the pan aside, covered for about 10 minutes.
8. Uncover the pan and with a fork, fluff the rice.
9. Serve immediately.

Nutritional Values:

Calories 270, Total Fat 5.8 g, Saturated Fat 3.2 g, Cholesterol 12 mg, Sodium 437 mg, Total Carbs 46.2 g, Fiber 1 g, Sugar 1 g, Protein 6.8 g

Buttered Quinoa

Preparation time: 10 minutes

Cooking time: 20 minutes

Total time: 30 minutes

Servings: 4

Ingredients:

- 1 cup quinoa, rinsed
- 1 tablespoon butter
- 2-3 teaspoons garlic powder
- Salt, as required
- 2 cups vegetable broth

How to Prepare:

1. Add all ingredients into a saucepan over medium-high heat and bring to a boil.
2. Now adjust the heat to low and simmer, covered for about 15 minutes.
3. Remove the saucepan of quinoa from heat and set aside, covered for about 5 minutes.
4. Uncover the pan and with a fork, fluff the quinoa.
5. Serve immediately.

Nutritional Values:

Calories 206, Total Fat 6.2 g, Saturated Fat 2.3 g, Cholesterol 8 mg, Sodium 443 mg, Total Carbs 28.8 g, Fiber 3.1 g, Sugar 0.7 g, Protein 8.7 g

SALADS

Summer isn't the only time for delicious and colorful salads. These salads combine the flavors of fall with the colors of summer for incredible dishes that are ready to be served at any gathering.

Citrus Salad	144
Chicken & Cranberry Salad	145
Chicken Caesar Salad	146
Bacon & Corn Salad	148
Cranberry & Spinach Salad	150
Beet & Walnut Salad	152
Fig Salad	154
Pork & Orange Salad	156
Steak & Pear Salad	157
Kale & Brussels Sprout Salad	158

Citrus Salad

Preparation time: 15 minutes

Total time: 15 minutes

Servings: 6

Ingredients:

- 8 clementines, peeled and cut in rounds
- 1 red grapefruit, peeled and cut in rounds
- 1 pink grapefruit, peeled and cut in rounds
- 1 navel orange, peeled and cut in rounds
- ½ cup pomegranate seeds
- ½ cup pistachios, chopped
- 2 teaspoons lime zest
- 3 tablespoons fresh lime juice
- 1 tablespoon honey

How to Prepare:

1. In a large-sized salad bowl, add all ingredients and gently toss to coat.
2. Serve immediately.

Nutritional Values:

Calories 118, Total Fat 2.7 g, Saturated Fat 0.3 g, Cholesterol 0 mg, Sodium 28 mg, Total Carbs 23.4 g, Fiber 3.8 g, Sugar 18.2 g, Protein 2.5 g

Chicken & Cranberry Salad

Preparation time: 15 minutes

Total time: 15 minutes

Servings: 5

Ingredients:

- 16 ounces cooked chicken, cut into bite-sized pieces
- ½ cup dried cranberries
- 3 cups celery stalks, chopped
- ¼ cup red onion, chopped
- ½ cup walnuts, chopped
- 1 cup mayonnaise
- 1 tablespoon fresh lemon juice
- 3 tablespoons balsamic vinegar
- Salt and ground black pepper, as required

How to Prepare:

1. In a large-sized salad bowl, add cooked chicken and remaining ingredients and mix well.
2. Serve immediately.

Nutritional Values:

Calories 418, Total Fat 26 g, Saturated Fat 3.5 g, Cholesterol 82 mg, Sodium 427 mg, Total Carbs 16 g, Fiber 2.4 g, Sugar 4.7 g, Protein 30.2 g

Chicken Caesar Salad

Preparation time: 20 minutes

Cooking time: 5 minutes

Total time: 25 minutes

Servings: 5

Ingredients:

Croutons

- 4 cups crusty bread, torn into ½-inch cubes
- ¼ cup extra-virgin olive oil
- ½ teaspoon lemon pepper
- Pinch of salt

Dressing

- ¼ cup Parmesan cheese, grated
- 2 tablespoons mayonnaise
- 2 tablespoons whole-milk yogurt
- 2 tablespoons white wine vinegar
- 1 tablespoon extra-virgin olive oil
- 2 teaspoons Dijon mustard
- 2 teaspoons Worcestershire sauce
- 2 green olives, pitted
- 1 large garlic clove, smashed
- Ground black pepper, as required

Salad

- 1 pound cooked chicken breast, cubed
- 1½ pounds romaine lettuce, torn
- ½ cup Parmesan cheese, shredded

How to Prepare:

1. For dressing: in a high-powered blender, add all ingredients and pulse until smooth.
2. For croutons: in a bowl, add all ingredients and toss to coat well.
3. Heat a 10-inch cast-iron wok over medium-high heat and cook the bread cubes for about 5 minutes, stirring continuously.
4. Remove the wok of bread cubes from the heat and set aside to cool.
5. In a bowl, add chicken, lettuce, croutons, and dressing and toss to coat well.
6. Top with cheese and serve.

Nutritional Values:

Calories 431, Total Fat 23.2 g, Saturated Fat 5.2 g, Cholesterol 81 mg, Sodium 517 mg, Total Carbs 21.3 g, Fiber 1.7 g, Sugar 3.8 g, Protein 34.2 g

Bacon & Corn Salad

Preparation time: 15 minutes

Cooking time: 18 minutes

Total time: 33 minutes

Servings: 8

Ingredients:

- 4 bacon slices, chopped
- 1 medium shallot, chopped
- 1 tablespoon fresh thyme
- 3 cups frozen corn, thawed
- 2 teaspoons sherry vinegar
- 1 teaspoon honey
- 10 cups fresh spinach, torn

How to Prepare:

1. Heat a small-sized cast-iron wok over medium-high heat and cook the bacon for about 8-10 minutes or until crisp.
2. With a spoon, transfer the cooked bacon onto a paper towel-lined plate to drain.
3. In the same wok, add the shallot and thyme and cook for about 2-3 minutes, stirring occasionally.
4. Add in the corn and vinegar and cook for about 4-5 minutes, tossing frequently.
5. Remove from heat and stir in honey and reserved bacon.
6. Set aside to cool.
7. In a salad bowl, add corn mixture and spinach and toss to coat well.
8. Serve immediately.

Nutritional Values:

Calories 143, Total Fat 6.9 g, Saturated Fat 2.1 g, Cholesterol 16 mg, Sodium 374 mg, Total Carbs 14.3 g, Fiber 2.5 g, Sugar 2.8 g, Protein 8.4 g

Cranberry & Spinach Salad

Preparation time: 15 minutes

Cooking time: 10 minutes

Total time: 25 minutes

Servings: 8

Ingredients:

Salad

- 1 tablespoon butter
- ¾ cup almonds, blanched and slivered
- 1 cup dried cranberries
- 1 pound fresh spinach, torn
- ½ cup feta cheese, crumbled

Dressing

- ½ cup vegetable oil
- ¼ cup cider vinegar
- ¼ cup white wine vinegar
- ½ cup white sugar
- 1 tablespoon poppy seeds
- 2 teaspoons onion, minced
- ¼ teaspoon paprika

How to Prepare:

1. In a medium-sized, non-stick frying pan, melt butter over medium heat and cook almonds for about 5-10 minutes, stirring frequently.
2. Remove the frying pan of almonds from heat and let them cool completely.
3. In a large-sized bowl, mix together the cranberries, spinach, and almonds.
4. In another small-sized bowl, add all dressing ingredients and beat until well blended.
5. Place the dressing over the salad and toss to coat well.
6. Top with feta and serve immediately.

Nutritional Values:

Calories 285, Total Fat 22.3 g, Saturated Fat 5.4 g, Cholesterol 12 mg, Sodium 170 mg, Total Carbs 18.6 g, Fiber 3 g, Sugar 14.2 g, Protein 5.1 g

Beet & Walnut Salad

Preparation time: 15 minutes

Cooking time: 1 hour

Total time: 1¼ hours

Servings: 4

Ingredients:

Salad

- 6 medium beets, scrubbed
- 6 cups fresh baby spinach
- 4 ounces feta cheese, crumbled
- ½ cup walnuts, toasted and chopped

Dressing

- ¼ cup extra-virgin olive oil
- 3 tablespoons balsamic vinegar
- 1 tablespoon maple syrup
- 2 teaspoons Dijon mustard
- Salt and ground black pepper, as required

How to Prepare:

1. Preheat your oven to 400°F.
2. Wrap each beet with a piece of foil.
3. Arrange wrapped beets onto a baking sheet and roast for 1 hour.
4. Remove the baking sheet of beets from oven and unwrap the beets.
5. Set aside to cool completely.
6. Then peel the beets and cut into pieces.
7. Meanwhile, for dressing: in a bowl, add all ingredients and beat until well blended.
8. In a salad bowl, add beets, spinach, walnuts, and dressing and toss to coat well.
9. Top with feta and serve.

Nutritional Values:

Calories 378, Total Fat 28.4 g, Saturated Fat 7.6 g, Cholesterol 22.9 mg, Sodium 537 mg, Total Carbs 22.9 g, Fiber 5.1 g, Sugar 16.5 g, Protein 11.7 g

Fig Salad

Preparation time: 15 minutes

Total time: 15 minutes

Servings: 2

Ingredients:

Salad

- 4 cups fresh greens, chopped
- 10 fresh figs, halved
- 1 cup red onion, sliced
- ¼ cup unsweetened coconut, shredded

Dressing

- 2 tablespoons balsamic vinegar
- 2 tablespoons tahini
- 1 teaspoon Dijon mustard
- 2 tablespoons fresh lemon juice
- ¼ teaspoon maple syrup
- ¼ teaspoon garlic powder
- Salt and ground black pepper, as required

How to Prepare:

1. For salad: in a large-sized salad bowl, add all ingredients.

2. For dressing: in a small-sized bowl, add all ingredients and beat until well blended.

3. Place dressing into salad bowl and toss to coat well.

4. Serve immediately.

Nutritional Values:

Calories 202, Total Fat 12.1 g, Saturated Fat 4.3 g, Cholesterol 0 mg, Sodium 176 mg, Total Carbs 21.1 g, Fiber 7.6 g, Sugar 6.4g, Protein 5.6 g

Pork & Orange Salad

Preparation time: 15 minutes

Total time: 15 minutes

Servings: 4

Ingredients:

- 1 pound cooked pork tenderloin, cut into slices
- 2 oranges, peeled and sectioned
- 1 red onion, sliced
- 3 cups butter lettuce, torn
- 3 cups fresh baby greens
- 2 tablespoons fresh orange juice
- 4 teaspoons olive oil
- 2 teaspoons sugar
- Salt and ground black pepper, as required

How to Prepare:

1. In a large-sized salad bowl, add all ingredients and toss to coat well.
2. Serve immediately.

Nutritional Values:

Calories 276, Total Fat 8.9 g, Saturated Fat 2 g, Cholesterol 83 mg, Sodium 71 mg, Total Carbs 17.9 g, Fiber 3.3 g, Sugar 13.1 g, Protein 31.3 g

Steak & Pear Salad

Preparation time: 15 minutes

Total time: 15 minutes

Servings: 4

Ingredients:

- ½ cup buttermilk
- 6 tablespoons mayonnaise
- 2 teaspoons cider vinegar
- Salt and ground black pepper, as required
- cooked flank steak, sliced
- 2 Bosc pears, cored and sliced
- 6 cups fresh baby arugula
- ½ cup pecans, toasted
- 1½ pounds

How to Prepare:

1. In a large-sized salad bowl, whisk together the buttermilk, mayonnaise, vinegar, salt, and black pepper.
2. Add the steak slices, pear, arugula, and pecans and toss to coat.
3. Serve immediately.

Nutritional Values:

Calories 412, Total Fat 18.7 g, Saturated Fat 3.7 g, Cholesterol 107 mg, Sodium 210 mg, Total Carbs 17.4 g, Fiber 3.6 g, Sugar 9.5 g, Protein 43.7 g

Kale & Brussels Sprout Salad

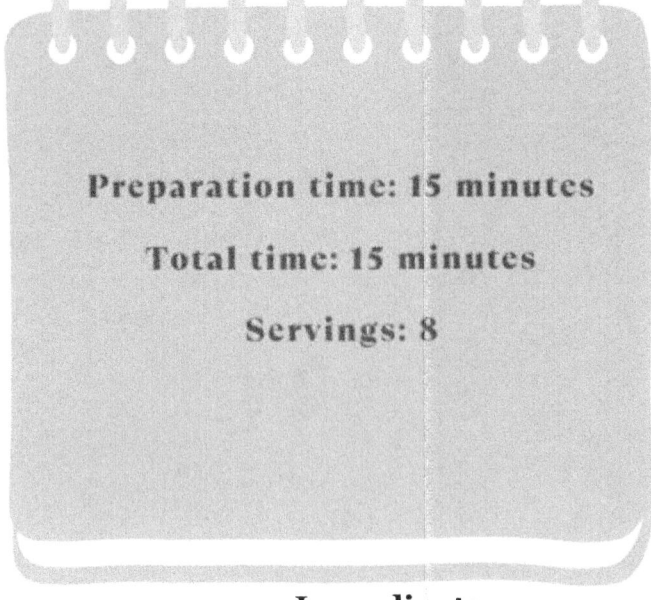

Preparation time: 15 minutes

Total time: 15 minutes

Servings: 8

Ingredients:

Salad

- 1½ pounds fresh kale, tough ribs removed and thinly sliced
- 14 ounces Brussels sprouts, trimmed and finely grated
- ½ cup almonds, toasted and chopped

Dressing

- 1 garlic clove, minced
- 1 tablespoon shallot, minced
- ¼ cup fresh lemon juice
- black pepper, as required
- ¼ cup olive oil
- Salt and ground

How to Prepare:

1. For salad: in a large-sized salad bowl, add all ingredients and mix.
2. For dressing: in a small-sized bowl, add all ingredients and beat until well blended.
3. Place dressing on salad and toss to coat well.
4. Serve immediately.

Nutritional Values:

Calories 155, Total Fat 9.5 g, Saturated Fat 1.3 g, Cholesterol 0 mg,

Sodium 70 mg, Total Carbs 15.2 g, Fiber 3.9 g, Sugar 1.5 g, Protein 5.6 g

BREADS

Bread is the classic carb that keeps our soul happy and our body warm throughout the cold winter months. It doesn't only make the house smell amazing; it also brings family and friends together to gather around the warm kitchen.

Dried Fruit Bread	160
Persimmon & Date Bread	162
Apple Bread	164
Chocolaty Banana Bread	166
Cranberry & Orange Bread	168
Cranberry & Pumpkin Bread	170
Pumpkin Bread	172
Chocolaty Pumpkin Bread	174
Zucchini & Carrot Bread	176
Braided Lemon Bread	178

Dried Fruit Bread

Preparation time: 15 minutes

Cooking time: 45 minutes

Total time: 1 hour

Servings: 16

Ingredients:

- 2 cups self-rising flour
- ½ cup plus 2 tablespoons granulated sugar
- 1 teaspoon baking powder
- 2/3 cup mixed dried fruit (cranberries, raisins, chopped apricots)
- ½ cup walnuts, chopped
- ¼ cup pumpkin seeds
- ¼ cup sunflower seeds
- 2 large eggs, beaten
- 1¼ cups plain yogurt
- 3 tablespoons sunflower oil
- 1 teaspoon vanilla extract

How to Prepare:

1. Preheat your oven to 350°F.
2. Line a bread loaf pan with lightly greased baking paper.
3. In a bowl, mix together flour, sugar, and baking powder.
4. Add the dried fruit, walnuts, and seeds and mix well.
5. In another bowl, add eggs, yogurt, oil, and vanilla extract and beat until well blended.
6. Add egg batter into flour mixture and mix until well blended.
7. Pour dough mixture into the prepared bread pan evenly.
8. Bake for approximately 41-45 minutes or until a wooden skewer inserted in the center comes out clean.
9. Remove bread pan from the oven and place onto a wire rack to cool for about 10 minutes.
10. Now, place the bread onto the wire rack to cool completely before slicing.
11. Cut into desired-sized slices and serve.

Nutritional Values:

Calories 194, Total Fat 7.3 g, Saturated Fat 1 g, Cholesterol 24 mg, Sodium 23 mg, Total Carbs 27.6 g, Fiber 1.2 g, Sugar 14.2 g, Protein 5.1 g

Persimmon & Date Bread

Preparation time: 15 minutes

Cooking time: 1 hour

Total time: 1¼ hours

Servings: 8

Ingredients:

- 1¾ cups almond flour, sifted
- 2 teaspoons baking powder
- 1 teaspoon baking soda
- ½ teaspoon ground ginger
- ½ teaspoon ground cinnamon
- ¼ teaspoon ground nutmeg
- Pinch of ground cloves
- ¼ teaspoon salt
- ½ cup maple syrup
- ½ cup unsweetened coconut milk
- 2 tablespoons coconut oil, melted
- ½ teaspoon fresh lemon juice
- 1 teaspoon vanilla extract
- 1 cup dates, peeled, pitted, and chopped
- 2 persimmons, peeled, cored, and chopped
- 1 cup walnuts, chopped

How to Prepare:

1. Preheat your oven to 350°F.
2. Place rack in the center of oven.
3. Line a bread loaf pan with lightly greased baking paper.
4. In a large-sized bowl, mix together flour, baking soda, baking powder, spices, and salt.
5. In another bowl, add maple syrup, coconut milk, oil, lemon juice, and vanilla extract and beat until well blended.
6. In the bowl of flour mixture, add the milk mixture and mix until well blended.
7. Gently fold in the dates, persimmon, and walnuts.
8. Pour dough mixture into the prepared bread pan evenly.
9. Bake for approximately 30 minutes.
10. Now, loosely, cover the bread pan with a piece of foil.
11. Bake for approximately 28-30 minutes more or until a wooden skewer inserted in the center comes out clean.
12. Remove the bread pan from oven and place onto a wire rack to cool for about 10 minutes.
13. Now, place the bread onto the wire rack to cool completely before slicing.
14. Cut into desired-sized slices and serve.

Nutritional Values:

Calories 434, Total Fat 28.1 g, Saturated Fat 7.6 g, Cholesterol 0 mg, Sodium 247 mg, Total Carbs 40.5 g, Fiber 5.9 g, Sugar 26.6 g, Protein 10 g

Apple Bread

Preparation time: 15 minutes

Cooking time: 1 hour

Total time: 1¼ hours

Servings: 10

Ingredients:

- 2 cup all-purpose flour
- 1 teaspoon baking powder
- 1 teaspoon ground cinnamon
- ¼ teaspoon ground cardamom
- ¼ teaspoon ground ginger
- Pinch of ground cloves
- ¼ teaspoon salt
- 2 cups sugar
- ½ cup canola oil
- 2 eggs
- 2 teaspoons vanilla extract
- 2 cups apples, peeled, cored and chopped

How to Prepare:

1. Preheat your oven to 350°F.
2. Grease a bread loaf pan.
3. In a large-sized bowl, mix together the flour, baking powder, spices, and salt.
4. In another bowl, add sugar, oil, and eggs and beat until well blended.
5. Add egg mixture into the bowl with flour mixture and mix until well blended.
6. Gently fold in chopped apples.
7. Pour the mixture into the bread pan evenly.
8. Bake for 45 minutes.
9. With a piece of foil, cover loaf pan and bake for 15 minutes more.
10. Remove the bread pan from oven and place onto a wire rack to cool for about 10 minutes.
11. Now, place the bread onto the wire rack to cool completely before slicing.
12. Cut into desired-sized slices and serve.

Nutritional Values:

Calories 377, Total Fat 12.1 g, Saturated Fat 1.1 g, Cholesterol 33 mg, Sodium 72 mg, Total Carbs 65.9 g, Fiber 1.9 g, Sugar 44.9 g, Protein 3.8 g

Chocolaty Banana Bread

Preparation time: 15 minutes

Cooking time: 35 minutes

Total time: 50 minutes

Servings: 12

Ingredients:

- ½ cup coconut flour
- ½ teaspoon baking powder
- ½ teaspoon baking soda
- ½ teaspoon ground cinnamon
- ¼ teaspoon salt
- 2 eggs, beaten lightly
- ¼ cup almond butter, melted
- 1 tablespoon maple syrup
- 4 medium ripe bananas, peeled and mashed
- ½ cup unsweetened dark chocolate chips

How to Prepare:

1. Preheat your oven to 350°F.
2. Lightly grease a 9x5-inch bread loaf pan.
3. In a large-sized bowl, mix together flour, baking powder, baking soda, cinnamon, and salt.
4. In another bowl, add egg, almond butter, and maple syrup and beat until well blended.
5. Add bananas to egg mixture and beat well.
6. In the bowl of flour mixture, add banana mixture and mix until well blended.
7. Gently fold in chocolate chips.
8. Pour the bread mixture into the prepared bread pan.
9. Bake for approximately 25-35 minutes or until a wooden skewer inserted in the center comes out clean.
10. Remove the bread pan from oven and place onto a wire rack to cool for about 10 minutes.
11. Now, place the bread onto the wire rack to cool completely before slicing.
12. Cut into desired-sized slices and serve.

Nutritional Values:

Calories 139, Total Fat 6.9 g, Saturated Fat 3.9 g, Cholesterol 27 mg, Sodium 117 mg, Total Carbs 16.4 g, Fiber 4.4 g, Sugar 5.9 g, Protein 3.4 g

Cranberry & Orange Bread

Preparation time: 15 minutes

Cooking time: 50 minutes

Total time: 1 hour 5 minutes

Servings: 12

Ingredients:

- 2 cups all-purpose flour
- 1½ teaspoons baking powder
- ½ teaspoon baking soda
- ¾ teaspoon salt
- 1 egg
- ¾ cup white sugar
- 2 tablespoons vegetable oil
- ¾ cup fresh orange juice
- 1 cup fresh cranberries, chopped
- ½ cup walnuts, chopped
- 1 tablespoon fresh orange zest, grated finely

How to Prepare:

1. Preheat your oven to 350°F.
2. Grease a 9x5-inch bread loaf pan.
3. In a large-sized bowl, mix together flour, baking powder, baking soda, and salt.
4. In another large bowl, add egg, sugar, oil, and orange juice and blend until well mixed.
5. In the bowl of flour mixture, add egg mixture and mix until well blended.
6. Fold in cranberries, walnuts, and orange zest.
7. Pour the dough mixture into the prepared loaf pan evenly.
8. Bake for 50 minutes or until a wooden skewer inserted in the center comes out clean.
9. Remove the bread pan from oven and place onto a wire rack to cool for about 10 minutes.
10. Now, place the bread onto the wire rack to cool completely before slicing.
11. Cut into desired-sized slices and serve.

Nutritional Values:

Calories 193, Total Fat 5.9 g, Saturated Fat 0.8 g, Cholesterol 14 mg, Sodium 206 mg, Total Carbs 31.8 g, Fiber 1.3 g, Sugar 14.3 g, Protein 4 g

Cranberry & Pumpkin Bread

Preparation time: 15 minutes

Cooking time: 1 hour

Total time: 1¼ hours

Servings: 10

Ingredients:

- 1 cup almond flour
- ½ cup coconut flour
- 1 teaspoon baking powder
- 1 teaspoon ground cinnamon
- ¾ teaspoon ground nutmeg
- ½ teaspoon salt
- ½ cup butter
- ¾ cup powdered sugar
- 6 large eggs (whites and yolks separated)
- 1 (15-ounce) can pumpkin puree
- ½ cup cream
- 8-10 drops liquid stevia
- ½ tablespoon vanilla extract
- 3 cups fresh cranberries, chopped
- ½ teaspoon cream of tartar
- 6 tablespoons egg white powder

How to Prepare:

1. Preheat your oven to 350°F.
2. Line a loaf pan with baking paper.
3. In a medium-sized bowl, add flours, baking powder, spices, and salt and mix well.
4. In another bowl, add the butter and sugar and beat until fluffy.
5. In the bowl of butter mixture, add the egg yolks, pumpkin, cream, stevia, and vanilla and beat until well blended.
6. In the bowl of butter mixture, add the flour mixture and beat until well blended.
7. Gently fold in the cranberries.
8. In a medium-sized, clean glass bowl, add the egg whites and cream of tartar.
9. With a high-speed electric mixer, beat the egg whites until very stiff.
10. Slowly, add the egg white powder, beating continuously until well blended.
11. Fold in the pumpkin bread mixture.
12. Place the dough mixture into the prepared bread pan evenly and with your hands, press to smooth the top surface.
13. Bake for approximately 56-60 minutes or until a wooden skewer inserted in the center comes out clean.
14. Remove the loaf pan from oven and place onto a wire rack to cool for about 10 minutes.
15. Then turn the loaf onto the wire rack to cool completely before slicing.
16. Cut the loaf into the desired-sized slices and serve.

Nutritional Values:

Calories 288, Total Fat 18.8 g, Saturated Fat 7.8 g, Cholesterol 138 mg, Sodium 288 mg, Total Carbs 19.7 g, Fiber 4.1 g, Sugar 12.7 g, Protein 10.7 g

Pumpkin Bread

Preparation time: 15 minutes

Cooking time: 1 hour

Total time: 1¼ hours

Servings: 24

Ingredients:

- 3 cups all-purpose
- flour
- 2 teaspoons baking soda
- ½ teaspoon baking powder
- 2 teaspoons pumpkin pie spice
- 1 teaspoon salt
- 3 eggs, beaten
- 2 cups white sugar
- 2/3 cups vegetable oil
- 2 cups pumpkin puree

How to Prepare:

1. Preheat your oven to 350°F.
2. Grease 2 9x5-inch bread loaf pans.
3. In a large-sized bowl, mix together flour, baking soda, baking powder, pumpkin pie spice, and salt.
4. In another bowl, add eggs, sugar, and oil and beat until well blended.
5. In the bowl of egg mixture, add pumpkin puree and beat until well blended.
6. In the bowl of flour mixture, add egg mixture and mix until well blended.
7. Pour the mixture into prepared bread pans evenly.
8. Bake for approximately 56-60 minutes or until a wooden skewer inserted in the center comes out clean.
9. Remove the bread pans from oven and place onto the wire racks to cool for about 10 minutes.
10. Now, place the breads onto the wire racks to cool completely before slicing.
11. Cut into desired-sized slices and serve.

Nutritional Values:

Calories 188, Total Fat 6.8 g, Saturated Fat 1.4 g, Cholesterol 20 mg, Sodium 210 mg, Total Carbs 30.4 g, Fiber 1 g, Sugar 17.4 g, Protein 2.5 g

Chocolaty Pumpkin Bread

Preparation time: 15 minutes

Cooking time: 1 hour

Total time: 1¼ hours

Servings: 36

Ingredients:

- 3½ cups all-purpose flour
- 2 teaspoons baking soda
- 1 tablespoon ground nutmeg
- 1 tablespoon ground cinnamon
- 1 teaspoon salt
- 4 eggs, beaten
- 1 cup vegetable oil
- 2/3 cups water
- 1 (15-ounce) can pumpkin puree
- 1 cup mini semisweet chocolate chips
- ½ cup walnuts, chopped

How to Prepare:

1. Preheat your oven to 350°F.
2. Grease and flour 3 (9x5-inch) loaf pans.
3. In a large-sized bowl, blend together flour, baking soda, and salt.
4. In another large-sized bowl, add eggs, sugar, oil, and water and beat until well blended.
5. In the bowl of egg mixture, add pumpkin puree and beat until well blended.
6. In the bowl of flour mixture, add pumpkin mixture and mix until well blended.
7. Gently fold in chocolate chips and walnuts.
8. Pour the mixture into the prepared bread pans evenly.
9. Bake for approximately 56-60 minutes or until a wooden skewer inserted in the center comes out clean.
10. Remove the bread pans from oven and place onto the wire racks to cool for about 10 minutes.
11. Now, place the breads onto the wire racks to cool completely before slicing.
12. Cut into desired-sized slices and serve.

Nutritional Values:

Calories 152, Total Fat 9.6 g, Saturated Fat 2.6 g, Cholesterol 18 mg, Sodium 145 mg, Total Carbs 14.7 g, Fiber 1.3 g, Sugar 3.6 g, Protein 2.5 g

Zucchini & Carrot Bread

Preparation time: 15 minutes

Cooking time: 58 minutes

Total time: 1 hour 13 minutes

Servings: 12

Ingredients:

- 1 cup all-purpose flour
- ½ teaspoon baking powder
- ½ teaspoon baking soda
- 2 teaspoons ground cinnamon
- Pinch of salt
- ½ cup light brown sugar
- ¼ cup granulated sugar
- 1 large egg
- 1/3 cup canola oil
- ¼ cup sour cream
- 2 teaspoons vanilla extract
- ½ cup zucchini, grated
- ½ cup carrot, peeled and grated
- ¼ cup walnuts, chopped
- ¼ cupraisins

How to Prepare:

1. Preheat your oven to 350°F.
2. Grease and flour a 9x5-inch bread loaf pan.
3. In a bowl, blend flour, baking powder, baking soda, cinnamon, and salt.
4. In another bowl, add sugars, egg, oil, sour cream, and vanilla extract and beat until well blended.
5. In the bowl of sugar mixture, add the flour mixture and mix until just combined.
6. Fold in zucchini, carrots, walnuts, and raisins.
7. Pour dough mixture into the bread pan evenly.
8. Bake for approximately 52-58 minutes or until a wooden skewer inserted in the center comes out clean.
9. Remove the bread pan from oven and place onto a wire rack to cool for about 10 minutes.
10. Now, place the bread onto the wire rack to cool completely before slicing.
11. Cut into desired-sized slices and serve.

Nutritional Values:

Calories 177, Total Fat 9.1 g, Saturated Fat 1.3 g, Cholesterol 18 mg, Sodium 77 mg, Total Carbs 22 g, Fiber 0.9 g, Sugar 12.3 g, Protein 2.6 g

Braided Lemon Bread

Preparation time: 20 minutes

Cooking time: 22 minutes

Total time: 42 minutes

Servings: 16

Ingredients:

- 1 (¼-ounce) packet active dry yeast
- ½ cup plus 1 teaspoon granulated sugar, divided
- ¼ cup plus 1 teaspoon warm water, divided
- 5 cups bread flour, divided
- 4 large eggs, divided
- ¾ cup warm whole milk
- ½ cup unsalted butter, softened
- 1 tablespoon fresh lemon juice
- 1 teaspoon lemon zest, grated
- 1 tablespoon poppy seeds

How to Prepare:

1. In the bowl of the stand mixer, hooked with a paddle attachment, add yeast, 1 teaspoon of sugar and ¼ cup of warm water and mix well.
2. Set aside for about 5 minutes or until foamy.
3. In the bowl of yeast mixture, add remaining sugar, 2 cups of flour, 3 eggs, milk, butter, lemon juice, and zest and beat on low speed until just combined.

4. Now, mix on medium speed, adding the remaining flour in small batches until well blended.
5. Set the speed of the mixer to medium-low and mix until dough pulls away from the sides.
6. Place the dough onto a lightly floured, smooth surface and sprinkle with poppy seeds.
7. With your clean hands, knead the dough until smooth and then shape into a ball.
8. Grease a.
9. Now place the dough ball into a greased glass bowl and turn to coat evenly.
10. With plastic wrap, cover the bowl and set aside at room temperature for about 1½ hours or until doubled in size.
11. Remove the dough from bowl and place onto a lightly floured surface.
12. Divide the dough into 2 equal-sized portions.
13. Cut 1 dough portion into 3 equal-sized portions and then shape each into a 15-inch-long rope.
14. Arrange the ropes about 1-inch apart and then braid together.
15. With your hands, pinch the ends of braid together and then tuck under.
16. Arrange the braided dough onto a baking paper-lined baking dish.
17. Repeat with the remaining dough portion.
18. With plastic wrap, cover the baking dish loosely and set aside at room temperature for about 1¼ hours or until doubled in size.
19. Preheat your oven to 375°F.
20. In a small-sized bowl, add the remaining egg and water and beat well.
21. Brush the top of each braided bread with egg mixture evenly.
22. Bake for approximately 22 minutes or until top of breads become golden brown.
23. Remove the baking dish of breads from the oven and place onto a wire rack to cool completely before serving.

Nutritional Values:

Calories 246, Total Fat 8 g, Saturated Fat 4.3 g, Cholesterol 63 mg, Sodium 64 mg, Total Carbs 37 g, Fiber 1.2 g, Sugar 7.2 g, Protein 6.3 g

STARTERS

Every great meal deserves a delicious start. The cold months mean more hearty flavors and starters designed to inspire your taste buds. Prepare for holiday or everyday meals with these incredible starters.

BACON-WRAPPED BRUSSELS SPROUTS	181
GLAZED MEATBALLS	182
BLACK BEAN MEATBALLS	184
BACON & CHEESE TRUFFLES	186
VEGGIE BALLS	188
PARMESAN SHRIMP	190
COCONUT SHRIMP	192
FRIED RAVIOLI	194
VEGGIE LATKES	196
JALAPENO POPPERS	198

Bacon-Wrapped Brussels Sprouts

Preparation time: 15 minutes

Cooking time: 40 minutes

Total time: 55 minutes

Servings: 6

Ingredients:

- 12 bacon slices
- 12 Brussels sprouts, trimmed

How to Prepare:

1. Preheat your oven to 400°F.
2. Line a baking sheet with baking paper.
3. Wrap each bacon slice around 1 Brussels sprout and then secure with toothpicks.
4. Place the wrapped Brussels sprouts onto the prepared baking sheet in a single layer.
5. Bake for approximately 40 minutes.
6. Serve warm.

Nutritional Values:

Calories 319, Total Fat 23.5 g, Saturated Fat 7.7 g, Cholesterol 62 mg, Sodium 937 mg, Total Carbs 4.3 g, Fiber 1.4 g, Sugar 0.8 g, Protein 22 g

Glazed Meatballs

Preparation time: 15 minutes

Cooking time: 1½ hours

Total time: 1¾ hours

Servings: 8

Ingredients:

Meatballs

- 1 pound lean ground beef
- 3 tablespoons onion, minced
- ½ cup breadcrumbs
- 1 egg, beaten
- 2 tablespoons water

Sauce

- 1 (8-ounce) can jellied cranberry sauce
- 1 tablespoon brown sugar
- ¾ cup chili sauce
- 1½ teaspoons fresh lemon juice

How to Prepare:

1. Preheat your oven to 350°F.
2. Grease a large-sized baking sheet.
3. For meatballs: in a large-sized bowl, add all ingredients and gently mix.
4. Make small, equal-sized balls from the mixture.
5. Arrange the rolled meatballs onto the prepared baking sheet in a single layer.
6. Bake for approximately 20-25 minutes.
7. In a large-sized saucepan, add all sauce ingredients over medium heat and bring to a gentle simmer.
8. Stir in meatballs and immediately adjust the heat to low.
9. Cover and simmer for about 1 hour.
10. Serve hot.

Nutritional Values:

Calories 164, Total Fat 4.5 g, Saturated Fat 1.6 g, Cholesterol 71 mg, Sodium 666 mg, Total Carbs 9.3 g, Fiber 1.5 g, Sugar 3 g, Protein 19 g

Black Bean Meatballs

Preparation time: 15 minutes

Cooking time: 12 minutes

Total time: 27 minutes

Servings: 8

Ingredients:

- 1 pound ground turkey
- 1 cup cooked black beans, mashed roughly
- 2 small bell peppers, seeded and chopped finely
- ½ cup fresh parsley, chopped
- Salt and ground black pepper, as required
- ¼ cup olive oil

How to Prepare:

1. In a large-sized bowl, add all ingredients except for oil and mix until well blended.
2. Make equal-sized balls from the mixture.
3. In a large-sized non-stick wok, heat oil over medium heat and cook the meatballs for about 5-7 minutes or until golden brown from all sides.
4. Cover the wok and cook for about 5 minutes more.
5. Serve hot.

Nutritional Values:

Calories 204, Total Fat 12.8 g, Saturated Fat 2 g, Cholesterol 58 mg, Sodium 83 mg, Total Carbs 7.6 g, Fiber 2.4 g, Sugar 1.5 g, Protein 17.8 g

Bacon & Cheese Truffles

Preparation time: 20 minutes

Total time: 20 minutes

Servings: 20

Ingredients:

Truffles

- ½ cup cooked bacon, chopped finely
- 1 (8-ounce) package cream cheese, softened
- ½ cup sharp cheddar cheese, shredded
- 2 tablespoons scallions, chopped
- 1 tablespoon dry ranch dressing mix

Coating

- ½ cup pecans, chopped and
- ½ cup cooked bacon, chopped

How to Prepare:

1. For truffles: in a medium bowl, add in all ingredients and with a hand mixer, mix well.

2. Make about 1½-inch balls from the mixture.

3. For coating: in a medium-sized shallow dish, blend together pecans and bacon.

4. Coat each ball with the pecan mixture evenly.

5. Arrange the truffles onto a baking paper-lined baking sheet and refrigerate for one hour before serving.

Nutritional Values:

Calories 128, Total Fat 11.4 g, Saturated Fat 4.7 g, Cholesterol 26 mg, Sodium 286 mg, Total Carbs 1 g, Fiber 0.4 g, Sugar 0.2 g, Protein 5.6 g

Veggie Balls

Preparation time: 15 minutes

Cooking time: 25 minutes

Total time: 40 minutes

Servings: 6

Ingredients:

- 2 medium-sized sweet potatoes, peeled and cubed
- 2 tablespoons unsweetened coconut milk
- 1 cup fresh spinach, chopped
- 1 medium shallot, chopped finely
- 1 teaspoon ground cumin
- ½ teaspoon granulated garlic
- ¼ teaspoon ground turmeric
- Salt and ground black pepper, as required
- ¼ cup ground flax seeds

How to Prepare:

1. Preheat your oven to 400°F.
2. Line a baking sheet with baking paper.
3. In a large-sized saucepan of water, arrange a steamer basket.
4. Place the sweet potato cubes into the steamer basket and steam for about 10-15 minutes.
5. In a large-sized bowl, place the sweet potato with coconut milk and mash well.
6. In the mashed sweet potato, add remaining ingredients except for flax seeds and mix until well blended.
7. Make about 1½-2-inch balls from the mixture.
8. Arrange the veggie balls onto the prepared baking sheet in a single layer.
9. Sprinkle with flax seeds.
10. Bake for approximately 20-25 minutes.
11. Serve hot.

Nutritional Values:

Calories 97, Total Fat 2.9 g, Saturated Fat 1.3 g, Cholesterol 0 mg, Sodium 38 mg, Total Carbs 15.7 g, Fiber 3.5 g, Sugar 0.6 g, Protein 2 g

Parmesan Shrimp

Preparation time: 20 minutes

Cooking time: 8 minutes

Total time: 28 minutes

Servings: 6

Ingredients:

- ¼ cup parmesan cheese, grated
- 2 tablespoons olive oil
- 4 garlic cloves, minced
- ½ teaspoon dried basil
- ½ teaspoon dried oregano
- Salt and ground black pepper, as required
- 1 pound medium shrimp, peeled and deveined
- 2 tablespoons fresh lemon juice

How to Prepare:

1. Preheat oven to 400°F.

2. Lightly grease a baking sheet.

3. Add parmesan, olive oil, garlic, herbs, salt, and black pepper and gently stir to combine.

4. Add shrimp and toss to coat well.

5. Arrange the shrimp onto the prepared baking sheet in a single layer.

6. Bake for approximately 6-8 minutes.

7. Remove the baking sheet of shrimp from oven and drizzle with lemon juice.

8. Serve immediately.

Nutritional Values:

Calories 165, Total Fat 8.8 g, Saturated Fat 2.3 g, Cholesterol 159 mg, Sodium 314 mg, Total Carbs 0.9 g, Fiber 0.1 g, Sugar 0.1 g, Protein 21.7 g

Coconut Shrimp

Preparation time: 20 minutes

Cooking time: 20 minutes

Total time: 40 minutes

Servings: 12

Ingredients:

- 3 eggs
- ½ cup panko breadcrumbs
- 1 teaspoon sugar
- 1 teaspoon garlic powder
- 1 teaspoon onion powder
- 1/8 teaspoon cayenne pepper
- Salt and ground white pepper, as required
- ½ cup unsweetened coconut flakes
- 24 medium raw shrimp, peeled and deveined

How to Prepare:

1. Preheat your oven to 425°F.
2. Line a large-sized baking sheet with baking paper.
3. In a small-sized shallow dish, crack the eggs and beat lightly.
4. In a second medium-sized shallow dish, mix together the remaining ingredients except for coconut and shrimp.
5. In a third medium shallow dish, place the coconut flakes.
6. First, dip each shrimp into eggs and then roll into the breadcrumb mixture.
7. Again, dip each shrimp into eggs and then roll into coconut flakes.
8. Spread the shrimp onto the baking sheet evenly.
9. Bake for approximately 15-20 minutes.
10. Serve warm.

Nutritional Values:

Calories 99, Total Fat 3.2 g, Saturated Fat 1.5 g, Cholesterol 134 mg, Sodium 135 mg, Total Carbs 2.8 g, Fiber 0.4 g, Sugar 0.6 g, Protein 11.8 g

Fried Ravioli

Preparation time: 20 minutes

Cooking time: 12 minutes

Total time: 32 minutes

Servings: 24

Ingredients:

- 6 eggs
- ½ cup half-and-half
- 2 cups all-purpose flour
- Salt and ground black pepper, as required
- 1 cup seasoned breadcrumbs
- 1 cup panko breadcrumbs
- 24 cheese raviolis
- 4 cups canola oil
- ¼ cup Parmesan cheese, shredded

How to Prepare:

1. In a small-sized shallow dish, whisk together the eggs and half-and-half.
2. In a second medium-sized shallow dish, whisk together the flour, salt, and black pepper.
3. In a third medium-sized shallow dish, stir together all the breadcrumbs.
4. First, dip each ravioli into egg mixture and then coat with flour mixture.
5. Again, dip into egg mixture and then coat with breadcrumbs.
6. In a large-sized, deep wok, heat the oil over medium heat and fry the raviolis in 6 batches for about 2 minutes or until golden brown.
7. With a slotted spoon, transfer the raviolis onto a paper towel-lined plate to drain.
8. With a slotted spoon, transfer the fried raviolis onto a serving platter and sprinkle with Parmesan cheese.
9. Serve warm.

Nutritional Values:

Calories 629, Total Fat 46.2 g, Saturated Fat 7.2 g, Cholesterol 78 mg, Sodium 268 mg, Total Carbs 39.8 g, Fiber 5.5 g, Sugar 4.1 g, Protein 14.5 g

Veggie Latkes

Preparation time: 15 minutes

Cooking time: 20 minutes

Total time: 35 minutes

Servings: 4

Ingredients:

- ¼ cup arrowroot powder
- 1 cup almond flour
- Salt and ground black pepper, as required
- 1 medium carrot, peeled and shredded
- 2 medium zucchinis, shredded
- 1 small red onion, chopped
- 2 small garlic cloves, minced
- 1 jalapeño pepper, chopped finely
- 2 eggs, beaten
- 2 tablespoons olive oil

How to Prepare:

1. For latkes: in a large-sized bowl, mix together arrowroot powder, almond flour, salt, and black pepper.

2. In the bowl of flour mixture, add remaining ingredients except for oil and mix until well blended.

3. Divide mixture into 8 equal-sized portions and shape into a patty.

4. In a large-sized non-stick wok, heat oil over medium heat and cook 2 latkes for about 2-3 minutes.

5. Flip the side and cook for about 2 minutes more.

6. Repeat with the remaining latkes.

7. Serve warm.

Nutritional Values:

Calories 319, Total Fat 23.4 g, Saturated Fat 2.7 g, Cholesterol 82 mg, Sodium 152 mg, Total Carbs 21.3 g, Fiber 5 g, Sugar 4.5 g, Protein 10.4 g

Jalapeno Poppers

Preparation time: 15 minutes

Cooking time: 15 minutes

Total time: 30 minutes

Servings: 6

Ingredients:

- ½ cup sharp cheddar cheese, shredded

- ½ cup cream cheese, softened

- 12 jalapeno peppers, halved lengthwise, seeds and membranes removed

- 12 bacon slices

How to Prepare:

1. Preheat oven to 400°F.

2. Line a medium-sized baking sheet with a piece of heavy-duty foil.

3. Mix cheddar cheese and cream cheese together in a bowl.

4. Stuff each jalapeno half with cheese mixture.

5. Arrange 2 halves back together and wrap with a slice of bacon.

6. Arrange bacon-wrapped peppers onto the prepared baking sheet.

7. Bake about 15 minutes.

8. Serve warm.

Nutritional Values:

Calories 420, Total Fat 33.7 g, Saturated Fat 14 g, Cholesterol 93 mg, Sodium 1537 mg, Total Carbs 3.5 g, Fiber 1.1 g, Sugar 1 g, Protein 25 g

SAUCES & STAPLES

It can't be winter cooking without tangy and tasty sauces to accompany all the incredible meals. Not only will the meal warm you, but the sauce will help bring warmth back to your soul.

Pumpkin Pie Spice 201
Cranberry Jam.. 202
Cranberry & Apple Relish 204
Cranberry Sauce 206
Fig & Raisins Chutney... 208
Raisin & Orange Chutney 210
BBQ Sauce.. 212
Mulling Spices 214
Spice Rub.. 215
Honey Mustard 216

Pumpkin Pie Spice

Preparation time: 5 minutes

Total time: 5 minutes

Servings: 3

Ingredients:

- 1 teaspoon ground cinnamon
- ¼ teaspoon ground ginger
- ¼ teaspoon ground nutmeg
- 1/8 teaspoon ground cloves

How to Prepare:

1. In a bowl, blend together all ingredients.
2. Store in an airtight jar.

Nutritional Values:

Calories 4, Total Fat 0.1 g, Saturated Fat 0.1 g, Cholesterol 0 mg, Sodium 0 mg, Total Carbs 0.9 g, Fiber 0.5 g, Sugar 0.1 g, Protein 0.1 g

Cranberry Jam

Preparation time: 15 minutes

Cooking time: 11 minutes

Canning time: 15 minutes

Total time: 41 minutes

Servings: 40

Ingredients:

- 1½ cups water

- 3 cups cranberries

- 2 cups bananas, peeled and mashed

- 1 teaspoon fresh lemon juice

- ½ of (6-fluid ounce) container liquid pectin

How to Prepare:

1. In a large-sized saucepan, mix water and cranberries over medium heat and simmer for about 10 minutes, stirring occasionally.
2. Stir in banana and cook for about 1 minute, stirring continuously.
3. Stir in lemon juice and pectin and remove from heat.
4. Transfer the jam to hot sterilized jars, filling up to about ¼-inch from the top.
5. Slide a small knife around the insides of each jar to remove air bubbles.
6. Wipe any trace of food off the rims of jars with a clean, moist kitchen towel.
7. Close each jar with a lid and screw on the ring.
8. Arrange the jars in a boiling water canner and process for about 10 minutes.
9. Remove the jars from the saucepan of water and place onto a wood surface several inches apart to cool completely.
10. After cooling with your finger, press the top of each jar's lid to ensure that the seal is tight.
11. The jam can be preserved in the pantry for up to 1 year.

Nutritional Values:

Calories 12, Total Fat 0 g, Saturated Fat 0 g, Cholesterol 0 mg, Sodium 0 mg, Total Carbs 2.6 g, Fiber 0.7 g, Sugar 1.2 g, Protein 0.1 g

Cranberry & Apple Relish

Preparation time: 15 minutes

Total time: 15 minutes

Servings: 16

Ingredients:

- 2 navel oranges

- 2 apples, peeled, cored and chopped

- 2 (12-ounce) packages cranberries

- 2 cups celery stalks, chopped

- 3 cups white sugar

How to Prepare:

1. Grate the peel of both oranges in a small-sized bowl. Set aside.

2. Discard the white membrane and seeds of oranges and cut into segments.

3. Divide the orange segments into 2 portions.

4. In a food processor, add 1 portion of oranges and half of the apples and cranberries and pulse until chopped coarsely.

5. Transfer the mixture into a large-sized bowl.

6. Now, pulse reaming fruit mixture and mix with the previous fruit mixture.

7. Add in the sugar and reserved orange peel and mix until well blended.

8. Cover and refrigerate to chill for at least 8 hours before serving.

Nutritional Values:

Calories 191, Total Fat 0.1 g, Saturated Fat 0 g, Cholesterol 0 mg, Sodium 10 mg, Total Carbs 48.3 g, Fiber 3 g, Sugar 44.3 g, Protein 0.4 g

Cranberry Sauce

Preparation time: 10 minutes

Cooking time: 15 minutes

Total time: 25 minutes

Servings: 16

Ingredients:

- 3 cinnamon sticks

- 5 whole allspice berries

- 5 whole cloves

- 1½ cups water

- 4 cups fresh cranberries

- 2 cups white sugar

How to Prepare:

1. In a spice bag, wrap the cinnamon, allspice berries and cloves.

2. In a pan, add spice bag, water and cranberries over medium heat and cook for about 9-10 minutes or until cranberries begin to burst.

3. Stir in sugar and immediately adjust the heat to low.

4. Cook for about 4-5 minutes or until sugar dissolves completely, stirring continuously.

5. Remove from heat and discard the spice bag.

6. Let the sauce cool completely.

7. Refrigerate to chill for about 8 hours before serving.

Nutritional Values:

Calories 111, Total Fat 0 g, Saturated Fat 0 g, Cholesterol 0 mg, Sodium 1 mg, Total Carbs 28.2 g, Fiber 1.5 g, Sugar 26 g, Protein 0 g

Fig & Raisins Chutney

Preparation time: 15 minutes

Cooking time: 1 hour 20 minutes

Total time: 1 hour 35 minutes

Servings: 24

Ingredients:

- 1/3 cup raisins
- ½ cup apple cider vinegar
- ½ cup brown sugar
- 2 cups fresh figs, stems removed and quartered
- 1/3 cup apple, cored and chopped
- ½ cup white onion, chopped
- ½ teaspoon ground ginger
- ¼ teaspoon ground nutmeg
- ¼ teaspoon ground clove
- 1/3 teaspoon salt

How to Prepare:

1. In a bowl of hot water, soak the raisins for 10 minutes.

2. Then drain the raisins and set aside.

3. In a saucepan, add vinegar and sugar over medium-low heat and cook for about 3-5 minutes or until sugar is dissolved completely, stirring continuously.

4. Add the raisins, figs, apple, onion, spices, and salt and bring to a boil.

5. Now adjust the heat to low and cook for about 1 hour, stirring occasionally.

6. Remove from the heat and transfer the chutney into jars.

Nutritional Values:

Calories 63, Total Fat 0.2 g, Saturated Fat 0 g, Cholesterol 0 mg, Sodium 34 mg, Total Carbs 15.9 g, Fiber 1.8g, Sugar 12.5 g, Protein 0.7 g

Raisin & Orange Chutney

Preparation time: 10 minutes

Cooking time: 25 minutes

Total time: 35 minutes

Servings: 8

Ingredients:

- 2 tablespoons flour
- 1 cup water
- 1 cup raisins
- 1 cup fresh orange juice
- 4 tablespoons sugar
- ¼ teaspoon salt
- Pinch of ground cloves

How to Prepare:

1. In a small-sized bowl, dissolve the flour in ½ cup of water. Set aside.

2. In a small-sized saucepan, add raisins, orange juice, and remaining water and bring to a boil.

3. Add the flour mixture, stirring continuously.

4. Add sugar, salt, and cloves and again, bring to a boil.

5. Now adjust the heat to low and simmer for about 10-15 minutes or until thickened, stirring occasionally.

6. Remove the saucepan of chutney from heat and set aside to cool before serving.

Nutritional Values:

Calories 98, Total Fat 0.2 g, Saturated Fat 0 g, Cholesterol 0 mg, Sodium 77 mg, Total Carbs 25.1 g, Fiber 0.8 g, Sugar 19.3 g, Protein 1 g

BBQ Sauce

Preparation time: 15 minutes

Cooking time: 1 hour

Total time: 1¼ hours

Servings: 12

Ingredients:

- 16 ounces low-sodium tomato sauce
- ½ cup apple cider vinegar
- 5 tablespoons honey
- 2 tablespoons tomato paste
- 1 tablespoon fresh lemon juice
- ½ tablespoon ground mustard
- ½ tablespoon onion powder
- ½ tablespoons ground black pepper
- 1 teaspoon paprika
- 1 cup water

How to Prepare:

1. In a medium saucepan, blend together all ingredients over medium-high heat and bring to a gentle boil.

2. Now adjust the heat to low and simmer for about 1 hour or until desired thickness.

3. Remove from heat and transfer into an airtight container.

4. Set aside to cool completely before storing in refrigerator.

Nutritional Values:

Calories 45, Total Fat 0.3 g, Saturated Fat 0 g, Cholesterol 0 mg, Sodium 203 mg, Total Carbs 10.5 g, Fiber 0.9 g, Sugar 9.4 g, Protein 0.9 g

Mulling Spices

Preparation time: 10 minutes

Total time: 10 minutes

Servings: 32

Ingredients:

- 3 ounces cinnamon sticks
- 1/3 cup cardamom pods
- ¼ cup star anise pods
- ¼ cup allspice berries
- ¼ cup whole cloves
- 1/3 cup dried orange peel
- ¼ cup black peppercorns

How to Prepare:

1. Place cinnamon sticks, cardamom pods, allspice berries, cloves, and star anise in a large zip-top bag.
2. With a rolling pin, crush the spices a few times.
3. Transfer the crushed spices into an airtight jar and stir in the orange peel and peppercorns.

Nutritional Values:

Calories 19, Total Fat 0.5 g, Saturated Fat 0.1 g, Cholesterol 0 mg, Sodium 3 mg, Total Carbs 4.7 g, Fiber 2.4 g, Sugar 0.1 g, Protein 0.5 g

Spice Rub

Preparation time: 5 minutes

Total time: 5 minutes

Servings: 20

Ingredients:

- ½ cup brown sugar
- ¼ cup paprika
- 1 tablespoon red chili powder
- 1 teaspoon cayenne pepper
- 1 tablespoon onion powder
- 1 tablespoon garlic powder
- 1 tablespoon dried onion
- 1 teaspoon ground cumin
- 1 tablespoon ground black pepper
- 1 tablespoon salt

How to Prepare:

1. In a bowl, blend together all ingredients.
2. Store in an airtight jar.

Nutritional Values:

Calories 23, Total Fat 0.3 g, Saturated Fat 0 g, Cholesterol 0 mg, Sodium 355 mg, Total Carbs 5.4 g, Fiber 0.8 g, Sugar 3.9 g, Protein 0.4 g

Honey Mustard

Preparation time: 5 minutes

Total time: 5 minutes

Servings: 16

Ingredients:

- ½ cup stone-ground mustard
- ¼ cup rice vinegar
- ¼ cup honey

How to Prepare:

1. In a small-sized bowl, add mustard, vinegar, and honey and beat until well blended.
2. Refrigerate before serving.

Nutritional Values:

Calories 42, Total Fat 1.4 g, Saturated Fat 0.1 g, Cholesterol 0 mg, Sodium 0 mg, Total Carbs 6.1 g, Fiber 0.7 g, Sugar 4.7 g, Protein 1.3 g

BAKING (cookies, cakes, pies, tarts)

Winter cooking can't be complete without cookies, cakes, pies, and tarts. The classic, delicious sweets bring friends and families together to gather in the kitchen. These sweet treats are sure to warm you, body and soul.

GINGERBREAD COOKIES	218
DOUBLE CHOCOLATE COOKIES	220
MERINGUE COOKIES	222
APPLE CAKE	224
CHOCOLATE PUMPKIN CAKE	226
CRANBERRY UPSIDE-DOWN CAKE	228
PUMPKIN PIE	230
CHOCOLATE TART	232
MINI ALMOND TARTS	234
APPLE PIE	236

Gingerbread Cookies

Preparation time: 15 minutes

Cooking time: 15 minutes

Total time: 30 minutes

Servings: 10

Ingredients:

- 1 cup almond flour
- ½ teaspoon baking powder
- ½ teaspoon baking soda
- 1 teaspoon ground ginger
- 1 teaspoon ground cinnamon
- ¼ teaspoon ground cloves
- ¼ teaspoon ground nutmeg
- ¼ teaspoon salt
- 3 tablespoons coconut oil, melted
- 2 tablespoons blackstrap molasses
- 1½ teaspoons vanilla extract

How to Prepare:

1. Preheat your oven to 350°F.
2. Arrange a rack in the center portion of oven.
3. Line a large-sized cookie sheet with baking paper.
4. In a large-sized bowl, add flour, baking powder, baking soda, spices, and salt and with a fork, mix well.
5. In another bowl, add oil, molasses, and vanilla extract and beat until well blended.
6. Add oil mixture in the bowl with flour mixture and mix until well blended.
7. With a tablespoon, place scoops of the mixture onto the prepared cookie sheet in a single layer about 2-inch apart.
8. With your hands, slightly flatten the cookies.
9. Bake for approximately 13-15 minutes or until top of cookies become golden brown.
10. Remove the cookie sheet from the oven and place onto the wire rack to cool for about 5 minutes.
11. Then turn the cookies onto the wire racks to cool completely before serving.

Nutritional Values:

Calories 118, Total Fat 9.4 g, Saturated Fat 4 g, Cholesterol 0 mg, Sodium 127 mg, Total Carbs 6 g, Fiber 1.5 g, Sugar 2.3 g, Protein 2.4 g

Double Chocolate Cookies

Preparation time: 15 minutes

Cooking time: 11 minutes

Total time: 26 minutes

Servings: 18

Ingredients:

- 2 large eggs
- 1 cup natural creamy almond butter
- 2 tablespoons peanut butter
- 1 tablespoon salted butter, melted
- 2/3 cup powdered sugar
- 2 tablespoons unsweetened cocoa powder
- 1 teaspoon baking soda
- 2 tablespoons water
- 1½ teaspoons vanilla extract
- ¼ cup unsweetened dark chocolate chips

How to Prepare:

1. Preheat your oven to 350°F.
2. Line a large-sized cookie sheet with baking paper.
3. In a large-sized bowl, add all the ingredients except chocolate chips and with an electric hand mixer, mix until well blended.
4. Fold in the chocolate chips.
5. Make about 1½-inch balls from the dough and place onto the prepared cookie sheet in a single layer about 2-inch apart.
6. With your palm, flatten each ball slightly.
7. Bake for approximately 8-11 minutes or until edges become golden brown.
8. Remove the cookie sheet from the oven and place onto a wire rack to cool for about 5 minutes.
9. Carefully turn the cookies onto the wire racks to cool completely before serving.

Nutritional Values:

Calories 164, Total Fat 11.5 g, Saturated Fat 3 g, Cholesterol 22 mg, Sodium 122 mg, Total Carbs 12.3 g, Fiber 2.1 g, Sugar 9.1 g, Protein 4.4 g

Meringue Cookies

Preparation time: 15 minutes

Cooking Time: 1¼ hours

Total Time: 1½ hours

Servings: 10

Ingredients:

- 3 large egg whites

- ½ teaspoon cream of tartar

- ¾ cup sugar

How to Prepare:

1. Preheat your oven to 200°F.
2. Line a large-sized cookie sheet with baking paper.
3. In a large-sized bowl, add egg whites and cream of tartar and with an electric mixer, beat on medium speed until frothy.
4. Add one spoon of sugar at a time and beat on medium speed until well blended. Keep adding the rest with constant beating.
5. Now, set the speed on high and beat until stiff peaks form.
6. Transfer whipped egg white mixture into a pastry bag, fitted with a large round tip.
7. Pipe 10 swirls onto the prepared cookie sheet about 1 ½-inch apart.
8. Bake for approximately 1-1¼ hours.
9. After baking time is completed, turn off your oven but do not open the door.
10. Allow the cookies in the oven to cool for about 1-2 hours before removing.
11. Remove cookie sheet of cookies from oven and place onto a wire rack to cool completely before serving.

Nutritional Values:

Calories 77, Total Fat 0 g, Saturated Fat 0 g, Cholesterol 0 mg, Sodium 13 mg, Total Carbs 19 g, Fiber 0 g, Sugar 18.8 g, Protein 1.4 g

Apple Cake

Preparation time: 15 minutes

Cooking time: 38 minutes

Total time: 53 minutes

Servings: 8

Ingredients:

Cake

- 1/3 cup coconut oil, melted and divided
- 2 medium apples, cored and chopped
- 1/3 cup maple syrup, divided
- ½ cup almond flour
- ½ cup coconut flour
- 1 teaspoon baking soda
- 1 teaspoon ground allspice
- 1 teaspoon ground cinnamon
- ½ teaspoon ground nutmeg
- Pinch of ground cloves
- ½ teaspoon salt
- 4 eggs
- ¼ cup unsweetened coconut milk
- 1 teaspoon vanilla extract
- ¾ cup raisins, chopped

Glaze

- ¼ cup unsweetened coconut milk
- ¼ cup coconut butter
- 2 tablespoons maple syrup
- 1 tablespoon palm shortening
- ½ teaspoon ground allspice

How to Prepare:

1. Preheat your oven to 375°F.
2. Grease and flour a Bundt cake pan.
3. Melt about 2 tablespoons of the coconut oil in a medium-sized frying pan over medium-high heat and cook apples for about 7-10 minutes.
4. Add in about 1 tablespoon of maple syrup and cook for about 2-3 minutes more.
5. Remove the frying pan of apples from heat and set aside to cool completely.
6. In a large-sized bowl, mix together flours, baking soda, spices, and salt.
7. In another bowl, add eggs, coconut milk, oil, vanilla extract, remaining oil, and maple syrup and beat well.
8. Add egg batter into the bowl of flour mixture and mix until well blended.
9. Fold in apples and raisins.
10. Pour cake mixture into the pan evenly.
11. Bake for approx. 20-25 minutes.
12. Remove cake pan from the oven once baked and then place onto a wire rack for about 10 minutes.
13. Carefully turn the cake onto the wire rack to cool completely before glazing.
14. Meanwhile, for glaze: in a high-speed blender, add all ingredients and pulse until well blended.
15. Spread glaze over cake and serve.

Nutritional Values:

Calories 375, Total Fat 24.8 g, Saturated Fat 16.6 g, Cholesterol 82 mg, Sodium 348 mg, Total Carbs 37.2 g, Fiber 4.7 g, Sugar 27.3 g, Protein 5.8 g

Chocolate Pumpkin Cake

Preparation time: 15 minutes

Cooking time: 40 minutes

Total time: 55 minutes

Servings: 10

Ingredients:

- 1 cup unsweetened dark chocolate chips
- 1/3 cup coconut oil, softened
- 1/3 cup coconut flour
- 2 tablespoons unsweetened coconut milk
- ¼ cup raw honey
- ¾ cup pumpkin puree
- 3 eggs
- ½ teaspoon ground nutmeg
- ½ teaspoon ground cinnamon
- ¼ teaspoon ground ginger

How to Prepare:

1. Preheat your oven to 350°F.
2. Grease an 8x8-inch glass baking dish
3. Place the chocolate chips in a microwave-safe bowl and microwave on Low for about 1 ½-2 minutes, stirring after every 30 seconds or until melted completely.
4. Remove the bowl of chocolate chips from the microwave and stir until smooth.
5. In the bowl of chocolate chips, add coconut oil, flour, and coconut milk and mix until a smooth mixture forms.
6. Set aside to cool completely.
7. In another bowl, add honey, pumpkin puree, eggs, and spices and beat until well blended.
8. Add the chocolate mixture into the bowl of egg mixture and mix until well blended.
9. Pour the cake mixture into the prepared cake pan evenly.
10. Bake for approximately 38-40 minutes or until a wooden skewer inserted in the center comes clean.
11. Cool the pan once baked on a wire rack for about 10 minutes.
12. Then turn the cake onto the wire rack to cool slightly before serving.
13. Cut the cake into desired-sized pieces and serve.

Nutritional Values:

Calories 282, Total Fat 22.3 g, Saturated Fat 15.5 g, Cholesterol 49 mg, Sodium 29 mg, Total Carbs 15.6g, Fiber 4.1 g, Sugar 7.8 g, Protein 5.2 g

Cranberry Upside-Down Cake

Preparation time: 15 minutes

Cooking time: 20 minutes

Total time: 35 minutes

Servings: 10

Ingredients:

Cranberry Sauce

- 2 cups fresh cranberries
- 1 tablespoon maple syrup
- 2 tablespoons lemon zest, grated very finely

Cake

- ½ cup coconut flour
- ½ teaspoon baking soda
- 2 teaspoons ground cinnamon
- ¼ teaspoon salt
- 3 eggs, beaten
- ¼ cup pure maple syrup
- 1/3 cup pumpkin puree
- 3 tablespoons unsweetened almond milk
- 1 teaspoon vanilla extract
- ½ cup pecans, chopped

How to Prepare:

1. Preheat your oven to 350°F.
2. Grease a 9-inch round cake pan.
3. For sauce: in a medium saucepan, add all ingredients over medium heat and cook for about 1-2 minutes or until cranberries start to pop, stirring continuously.
4. Remove from the heat and place the cranberry sauce into the prepared cake pan.
5. Meanwhile, in a medium-sized bowl, mix together flour, baking soda, cinnamon, and salt.
6. In another bowl, add eggs, pumpkin puree, maple syrup, almond milk, and vanilla extract and beat until well blended.
7. In the bowl of flour mixture, add the egg mixture and mix until just blended.
8. Gently fold in the chopped pecans.
9. Now pour the cake mixture over the cranberry sauce evenly.
10. Bake for approximately 16-20 minutes or until a wooden skewer inserted in the center of cake comes out clean.
11. Remove the pan from the oven and place over a wire rack to cool for about 10 minutes.
12. Carefully invert the cake over a serving platter and set aside to cool completely before serving.
13. Cut the cooled cake into desired-sized slices and serve.

Nutritional Values:

Calories 90, Total Fat 6.2 g, Saturated Fat 1 g, Cholesterol 49 mg, Sodium 145 mg, Total Carbs 6 g, Fiber 2.3 g, Sugar 2.7 g, Protein 2.6 g

Pumpkin Pie

Preparation time: 15 minutes

Cooking time: 40 minutes

Total time: 55 minutes

Servings: 8

Ingredients:

- 1 cup packed brown sugar
- 2 teaspoons ground cinnamon
- 1 teaspoon ground ginger
- ½ teaspoon salt
- 1 (15-ounce) can pumpkin puree
- 2 tablespoons molasses
- 1 cup evaporated milk
- 3 eggs, beaten
- 1 (9-inch) single pie crust

How to Prepare:

1. Preheat your oven to 425°F.

2. Grease a pie dish.

3. Arrange the pie crust into the prepared pie dish and bake for approximately 8-10 minutes.

4. Remove the pie dish of crust from oven and set aside to cool slightly.

5. In a large-sized bowl, mix together brown sugar, spices, and salt.

6. Add in pumpkin puree, molasses, evaporated milk, and eggs and mix until well blended.

7. Pour the mixture over pie crust evenly.

8. Bake for approximately 38-40 minutes or until pie filling is set completely.

9. Remove the pie from the oven and set aside to cool completely before serving.

Nutritional Values:

Calories 231, Total Fat 7.3 g, Saturated Fat 2.7 g, Cholesterol 71 mg, Sodium 285 mg, Total Carbs 37.9 g, Fiber 2.1 g, Sugar 30.2 g, Protein 5.4 g

Chocolate Tart

Preparation time: 20 minutes

Cooking time: 5 minutes

Total time: 25 minutes

Servings: 8

Ingredients:

Crust

- 1 ¼ cups almond flour
- ¼ cup powdered sugar
- ¼ cup unsweetened cocoa powder
- 5 tablespoons butter, melted

Filling

- ¾ cup milk
- ¾ cup whipping cream
- ¼ cup butter
- 1/3 cup powdered sugar
- 3 ounces dark chocolate, chopped
- 3 tablespoons unsweetened cocoa powder
- ½ teaspoon espresso powder
- 3 large eggs

Topping

- 1 cup fresh strawberries, sliced

How to Prepare:

1. For crust: lightly grease a 9-inch tart pan with a removable bottom.
2. In a bowl, add all ingredients and mix until well blended.
3. Place the crust mixture into the prepared tart pan and, with your hands, press the mixture into the bottom and up the sides.
4. Refrigerate until use.
5. For filling: in a small-sized pan, add almond milk, cream, and butter and bring to a boil stirring constantly.
6. Immediately, remove from heat.
7. In a blender, add sugar, chocolate, cocoa powder, and espresso powder and pulse until well blended.
8. Add cream mixture and pulse until smooth.
9. Add eggs and pulse until smooth.
10. Pour the chocolate mixture over the crust evenly and refrigerate for about 2 hours.
11. Gently and carefully press the tart pan from the bottom to remove the sides.
12. Transfer the tart onto a platter.
13. Refrigerate for about 15-20 minutes before serving.
14. Garnish with strawberry slices and serve.

Nutritional Values:

Calories 398, Total Fat 31.4 g, Saturated Fat 14.5 g, Cholesterol 121 mg, Sodium 143 mg, Total Carbs 25.5 g, Fiber 4.2 g, Sugar 18 g, Protein 9.1 g

Mini Almond Tarts

Preparation time: 15 minutes

Cooking Time: 25 minutes

Total Time: 40 minutes

Servings: 12

Ingredients:

Tart Shells

- ¼ cup white sugar
- 1/3 cup butter, softened
- 1 cup all-purpose flour

Filling

- ¼ cup brown sugar
- 1/3 cup almonds, slivered
- 2 tablespoons butter, softened
- 2 teaspoons all-purpose flour
- 1½ tablespoons cream

How to Prepare:

1. Preheat your oven to 350°F.
2. Grease a 12 cups muffin pan.
3. For tart shells: in a bowl, add sugar and butter and beat until smooth and creamy.
4. Slowly add flour, beating continuously until a smooth dough forms.
5. Place the mixture into the prepared muffin cups evenly.
6. With your fingers, press the dough into the bottom and up the sides.
7. For filling: in a small-sized pan, blend together brown sugar, almonds, and butter over medium heat.
8. Stir in flour and cream and bring to a gentle boil, stirring continuously.
9. Cook for about 10 minutes, stirring continuously.
10. Remove the pan of filling from heat and let it cool slightly.
11. Pour the filling mixture in the prepared tart shells evenly.
12. Bake for approximately 10-15 minutes.
13. Remove from oven and set aside for 10-15 minutes.
14. Carefully remove each tart from muffin cups and serve.

Nutritional Values:

Calories 144, Total Fat 8.5 g, Saturated Fat 4.6 g, Cholesterol 19 mg, Sodium 52 mg, Total Carbs 15.5 g, Fiber 0.6 g, Sugar 7.3 g, Protein 1.7 g

Apple Pie

Preparation time: 25 minutes

Cooking time: 55 minutes

Total time: 1 hour 20 minutes

Servings: 14

Ingredients:

Crust

- 2 cups whole-wheat pastry flour
- ½ teaspoon salt
- 12 tablespoons cold unsalted butter, cubed
- 8-10 tablespoons ice water
- 1 tablespoon apple cider vinegar

Filling

- 6 cups sweet apples, peeled, cored and cut into ¼-inch slices
- 1/3 cup plus 1 tablespoon white sugar
- 2 tablespoons tapioca flour
- 1 tablespoon ground cinnamon
- 1 tablespoon fresh lemon juice
- 1 teaspoon vanilla extract

Egg Wash

- 1 egg
- 1 tablespoon milk

How to Prepare:

1. For crust: in a large-sized bowl, blend together the flour and salt.
2. With 2 forks, cut in butter until a crumbly mixture forms.
3. Slowly add 5 tablespoons of the ice water and with a wooden spoon mix well.
4. In the bowl of flour mixture, add the remaining ice water and vinegar and mix until a dough comes together.
5. Now shape the dough into a flat square by pressing with hands or using a rolling pin.
6. Then cut the dough in 2 portions.
7. Again, shape each dough portion into a disc.
8. With plastic wrap, wrap each dough disc tightly and refrigerate for 2 hours.
9. For filling: in a bowl, add the apple slices and remaining ingredients and toss to coat well. Set aside for about 20-30 minutes.
10. Preheat your oven to 400°F.
11. Place 1 chilled dough disc onto a lightly floured surface and sprinkle the top with a little flour.
12. Roll the dough using a flour dusted rolling pin into a 12-inch circle.
13. Arrange the dough circle into the pie plate and with your hands, gently press it down and up the sides of the plate.
14. Arrange the apple slices over the crust.
15. Spoon 2 tablespoons of the leftover juices over the filling.
16. Now, place the second chilled dough disc onto a lightly floured surface and sprinkle the top with a little flour.
17. With a lightly floured rolling pan, roll the second dough disc into a 12-inch circle.
18. Cut the rolled dough circle into equal-sized strips.
19. Arrange the dough strips on top of the pie in a woven lattice pattern.
20. For egg wash: In a small-sized bowl, add egg and milk and beat well.
21. Coat the top of dough strips with the egg wash lightly.
22. Arrange the pie dish onto a large-sized baking sheet and bake for approximately 20 minutes.
23. Remove the pie from the oven and set the temperature of the oven to 375°F.
24. With a large-sized piece of foil, cover the pie plate and bake for approximately 30-35 minutes further.
25. Remove the pie from the oven and cool onto a wire rack completely before serving.
26. Cut into desired-sized slices and serve.

Nutritional Values:

Calories 236, Total Fat 10.6 g, Saturated Fat 6.4 g, Cholesterol 38 mg,

Sodium 158 mg, Total Carbs 34.3 g, Fiber 3.1 g, Sugar 16.1 g, Protein 2.7 g

DESSERTS

Delectable, winterized desserts can help warm your soul. Though they may not contain hearty vegetables and wild spices, these desserts are sure to bring your loved ones into the kitchen for a bite.

Strawberry & Banana Trifle 239
No-Bake Banana Pudding 240
Cranberry & Orange Mousse 242
Pumpkin Crème Brûlée 244
Chocolate Custard 246
Orange Cupcakes 248
Pumpkin Brownies 250
Cranberry, Apple & Pear Crisp 252
Bread & Raisins Pudding 254
Stuffed Apples 256

Strawberry & Banana Trifle

Preparation time: 15 minutes

Total time: 15 minutes

Servings: 12

Ingredients:

- 3 cups cold milk
- 1 (5-ounce) package instant vanilla pudding mix
- 1 (9-inch) angel food cake, cubed
- 4 medium bananas, peeled and sliced
- 1 (16-ounce) package frozen strawberries, thawed
- 1 (12-ounce) container frozen whipped topping, thawed
- ½ cup fresh strawberries, hulled and sliced

How to Prepare:

1. With the help of the milk, prepare the pudding mix according to the package's directions.
2. In a serving trifle bowl, place a row of half of the cake cubes, followed by half of the pudding, banana, frozen strawberries, and whipped topping.
3. Repeat the layers in the same order.
4. Cover and refrigerate for 4 hours.
5. Garnish with fresh strawberries and serve.

Nutritional Values:

Calories 239, Total Fat 8.3 g, Saturated Fat 5 g, Cholesterol 28 mg,

Sodium 312 mg, Total Carbs 37.9 g, Fiber 2.3 g, Sugar 14.5 g, Protein 5.4 g

No-Bake Banana Pudding

Preparation time: 15 minutes

Total time: 15 minutes

Servings: 12

Ingredients:

- 1 (8-ounce) package cream cheese, softened
- 1 (5-ounce) package instant vanilla pudding mix
- 3 cups cold milk
- 1 (14-ounce) can sweetened condensed milk
- 1 teaspoon vanilla extract
- ½ pound frozen whipped topping, thawed completely and divided
- ½ of (12-ounces) package vanilla wafers
- 4 medium bananas, peeled and sliced

How to Prepare:

1. In a large-sized bowl, add cream cheese and beat until fluffy.

2. Add in the vanilla pudding mix, milk, condensed milk, and vanilla extract and beat until well blended and smooth.

3. Fold in 4 ounces of whipped topping.

4. Arrange the wafers in the bottom of a 13x9-inch sized baking dish evenly.

5. Place sliced bananas over the wafers evenly.

6. Place cream cheese mixture over banana slices evenly.

7. Place remaining whipped topping over cream cheese mixture evenly.

8. Refrigerate to chill before serving.

Nutritional Values:

Calories 363, Total Fat 17.5 g, Saturated Fat 10.1 g, Cholesterol 60 mg, Sodium 230mg, Total Carbs 45.6 g, Fiber 1.3 g, Sugar 34.6 g, Protein 8.1 g

Cranberry & Orange Mousse

Preparation time: 10 minutes

Cooking time: 2 minutes

Total time: 12 minutes

Servings: 4

Ingredients:

- 1 cup unsweetened coconut milk
- 8 ounces fresh cranberries
- ¼ cup honey
- 3 tablespoons fresh orange juice
- 1 teaspoon vanilla extract
- 1 tablespoon grass-fed gelatin
- 2 teaspoons fresh orange zest, grated very finely

How to Prepare:

1. Add coconut milk and cranberries in a high-speed blender and pulse until smooth.

2. Add honey, orange juice, and vanilla and pulse until well blended.

3. Through a fine sieve, strain the mixture into a pan over medium heat.

4. Cook for about 2 minutes, stirring continuously.

5. Remove from the heat.

6. Slowly add gelatin and stir until dissolved completely, stirring continuously.

7. Fold in orange zest.

8. Transfer the mixture into 4 serving bowls

9. Refrigerate to set before serving.

Nutritional Values:

Calories 249, Total Fat 14.3 g, Saturated Fat 12.7 g, Cholesterol 0 mg, Sodium 13 mg, Total Carbs 27.5 g, Fiber 3.6 g, Sugar 22.6 g, Protein 3 g

Pumpkin Crème Brûlée

Preparation time: 15 minutes

Cooking time: 45 minutes

Total time: 1 hour

Servings: 8

Ingredients:

- 3 tablespoons powdered sugar
- 4 large egg yolks
- 1 cup heavy cream
- ½ cup milk
- ½ cup pumpkin puree
- ½ teaspoon vanilla extract
- ½ teaspoon pumpkin pie spice
- ¼ teaspoon salt
- 4 teaspoons granulated sugar

How to Prepare:

1. Preheat your oven to 300°F.
2. Arrange 8 ramekin dishes in a large baking dish.
3. In a bowl, add powdered sugar and egg yolks and beat until a slightly thick mixture forms. Set aside.
4. In a small-sized pan, add cream and milk over medium-high heat and cook until just beginning to bubble, stirring frequently.
5. Remove from the heat.
6. Slowly, add the egg mixture into cream mixture, beating continuously until well blended.
7. Add pumpkin puree, vanilla extract, pumpkin pie spice, and salt and beat until well blended.
8. Transfer the mixture into the ramekins about ¾ of the way full.
9. Add boiling water in the baking dish, about halfway up the side of the ramekins.
10. Bake for approximately 30-40 minutes.
11. Remove from oven and transfer the ramekins into the refrigerator for at least 4 hours.
12. Just before serving, sprinkle the ramekins with granulated sugar evenly.
13. Holding a kitchen torch about 4-5-inch from top caramelize the sugar for about 2 minutes.
14. Set the ramekins aside for about 8-10 minutes before serving.

Nutritional Values:

Calories 112, Total Fat 8.2 g, Saturated Fat 4.5 g, Cholesterol 127 mg, Sodium 91 mg, Total Carbs 7.8 g, Fiber 0.5 g, Sugar 6.3 g, Protein 2.3 g

Chocolate Custard

Preparation time: 15 minutes

Cooking time: 35 minutes

Total time: 50 minutes

Servings: 6

Ingredients:

- 2½ cups plus 2 tablespoons milk
- 5 large eggs
- ½ cup honey
- 1 tablespoon vanilla extract
- 3 tablespoons unsweetened cocoa powder
- 2 tablespoons hot water
- Pinch of ground cinnamon

How to Prepare:

1. Preheat your oven to 325°F.
2. Grease a casserole dish.
3. In a bowl, add milk, eggs, and honey and beat until well blended.
4. In a small-sized bowl, add cocoa powder and hot water and mix until a paste forms.
5. Add the choco paste into the egg mixture and stir to combine.
6. Pour the custard mixture into the prepared casserole dish evenly.
7. Sprinkle with cinnamon and nutmeg.
8. Arrange the casserole dish in a large baking dish.
9. Carefully pour boiling water into the baking dish to about halfway up the side of the casserole dish.
10. Bake for approx. 35 minutes.
11. Serve warm.

Nutritional Values:

Calories 208, Total Fat 6.5 g, Saturated Fat 2.7 g, Cholesterol 163 mg, Sodium 107 mg, Total Carbs 30.3 g, Fiber 1 g, Sugar 288.3 g, Protein 9.1 g

Orange Cupcakes

Preparation time: 15 minutes

Cooking time: 20 minutes

Total time: 45 minutes

Servings: 18

Ingredients:

Cupcakes

- 2 cups gluten-free all-purpose flour
- ½ teaspoon baking soda
- 1 teaspoon baking powder
- ½ teaspoon ground cinnamon
- 1 tablespoon orange zest, grated
- ¼ teaspoon salt
- 2 eggs
- ½ cup olive oil
- 1 cup sugar
- 1 teaspoon vanilla extract
- 1 teaspoon orange extract
- 1/3 cup fresh orange juice

Frosting

- 1/3 cup unsalted butter
- 1/3 cup fresh orange juice
- 1 cup powdered sugar
- 4 tablespoons heavy cream

How to Prepare:

1. Preheat your oven to 350°F.
2. Line 18 cups of 2 standard-sized muffin tins with paper liners.
3. For cupcakes: in a large-sized bowl, combine flour, baking powder, cinnamon, orange zest, and salt.
4. Add eggs, oil, sugar, vanilla, orange extract, and orange juice and with an electric mixer on medium speed, mix until well blended.
5. Pour the mixture into the papered muffin cups.
6. Bake for approximately 25-30 minutes or until a wooden skewer inserted in the center comes out clean.
7. Remove the muffin tin from the oven and place onto a wire rack to cool for about 10 minutes.
8. Carefully invert the cupcakes onto a wire rack to cool completely before frosting.
9. Meanwhile, for frosting: in a bowl, add butter, orange juice, sugar and heavy cream and mix with a hand mixer until smooth.
10. Spread frosting over each cupcake evenly and serve.

Nutritional Values:

Calories 217, Total Fat 11 g, Saturated Fat 3.9 g, Cholesterol 32 mg, Sodium 99 mg, Total Carbs 29 g, Fiber 1.4 g, Sugar 18.6 g, Protein 2.1 g

Pumpkin Brownies

Preparation time: 15 minutes

Cooking time: 40 minutes

Total time: 55 minutes

Servings: 9

Ingredients:

- 1 tablespoon ground flax seed
- 2 tablespoons water
- ½ cup almond butter
- ½ cup pumpkin puree
- ¼ cup maple syrup
- ¼ cup unsweetened
- cocoa powder
- 2 teaspoons vanilla extract
- ½ teaspoon baking soda
- ½ tablespoon pumpkin pie spice
- ½ teaspoon salt
- ¼ cup dark chocolate chips

How to Prepare:

1. Preheat your oven to 350°F.
2. Line a 6×6-inch baking dish with baking paper.
3. In the bowl of a food processor, add all the ingredients except the chocolate chips and pulse until smooth.
4. Now place the mixture into a large-sized bowl and gently stir in chocolate chips.
5. In the bottom of the prepared baking dish, pour the brownie mixture evenly.
6. With a spatula, smooth the top surface.
7. Bake for approximately 38-40 minutes or until a wooden skewer inserted in the center comes out clean.
8. Remove the baking dish with the brownie from the oven and place onto a wire rack to cool completely before cutting.
9. With a knife, cut the brownie into desired-sized squares and serve.

Nutritional Values:

Calories 61, Total Fat 2 g, Saturated Fat 0.8 g, Cholesterol 0 mg, Sodium 201 mg, Total Carbs 11 g, Fiber 1.5 g, Sugar 7.7 g, Protein 1.2 g

Cranberry, Apple & Pear Crisp

Preparation time: 15 minutes

Cooking time: 45 minutes

Total time: 1 hour

Servings: 8

Ingredients:

Filling

- ½ cup dried cranberries
- 2 pears, peeled, cored and cubed
- 2 apples, peeled, cored and cubed
- 1 tablespoon all-purpose flour
- 1½ tablespoon fresh lemon juice
- 2 tablespoons honey

Topping

- ½ cup all-purpose flour
- ¼ cup ground walnuts
- ½ cup quick-cooking oats
- ½ cup packed brown sugar
- ½ cup butter

How to Prepare:

1. Preheat your oven to 375°F.

2. Lightly grease an 8-inch round baking dish.

3. For filling: in a medium-sized bowl, blend together all ingredients.

4. For topping: in another bowl, add all ingredients and mix until coarse crumb forms.

5. In the prepared baking dish, pour the filling mixture evenly and top with crumb mixture.

6. Bake for approximately 45 minutes or until golden brown in color.

7. Serve warm.

Nutritional Values:

Calories 272, Total Fat 14.4 g, Saturated Fat 7.5 g, Cholesterol 31 mg, Sodium 87 mg, Total Carbs 35.1 g, Fiber 4.2 g, Sugar 201 g, Protein 2.9 g

Bread & Raisins Pudding

Preparation time: 15 minutes

Cooking time: 45 minutes

Total time: 1 hour

Servings: 12

Ingredients:

- 6 (day-old) bread slices, torn into small pieces
- 2 tablespoons butter, melted
- ½ cup black raisins
- 2 cups milk
- 4 eggs, beaten
- ¾ cup white sugar
- 1 teaspoon vanilla extract
- 1 teaspoon ground cinnamon

How to Prepare:

1. Preheat your oven to 350°F.

2. Lightly grease a square baking dish.

3. Place the torn bread in the bottom of the prepared baking dish.

4. Drizzle with butter and top with raisins evenly.

5. In a medium-sized bowl, add in remaining ingredients and mix until well blended.

6. Pour the egg mixture over the raisins evenly.

7. Bake for approximately 43-45 minutes or until top becomes golden brown.

8. Serve warm.

Nutritional Values:

Calories 140, Total Fat 4.5 g, Saturated Fat 2.2 g, Cholesterol 63 mg, Sodium 91 mg, Total Carbs 22.2 g, Fiber 0.5 g, Sugar 18.3 g, Protein 3.8 g

Stuffed Apples

Preparation time: 10 minutes

Cooking time: 40 minutes

Total time: 50 minutes

Servings: 2

Ingredients:

- 2 small apples, top removed
- 2-3 tablespoons rolled oats
- 2 tablespoons almonds, chopped
- 3-4 drops liquid stevia
- Pinch of ground cinnamon
- ½-¾ cup water

How to Prepare:

1. Preheat your oven to 350°F.

2. With a small scooper, scoop out the flesh from inside the apple.

3. In a small-sized bowl, blend together the remaining ingredients except for water.

4. Stuff the apples with the oat mixture evenly.

5. Arrange the apples into a small baking dish.

6. Add water into the baking dish around the apples.

7. Bake for approximately 30-40 minutes.

8. Serve warm.

Nutritional Values:

Calories 170, Total Fat 3.7 g, Saturated Fat 0.3 g, Cholesterol 0 mg, Sodium 2 mg, Total Carbs 35.6 g, Fiber 6.7 g, Sugar 23.5 g, Protein 2.5 g

WARM AROMATIC TEAS

What is more warming and comforting on a cold day than a hot cup of tea? All of these recipes will help keep you warm and fill your house with incredible aromas.

JUNIPER BERRY TEA	259
ORANGE TEA	260
MINT GREEN TEA	261
LEMONY GINGER TEA	262
LEMONY GREEN TEA	263
GINGER & TURMERIC TEA	264
PASSION FRUIT TEA	265
SPICED MILK TEA	266
APPLE TEA	267
CRANBERRY TEA	268

Juniper Berry Tea

Preparation time: 5 minutes

Cooking time: 10 minutes

Total time: 15 minutes

Servings: 1

Ingredients:

- 1 teaspoon dried juniper berries, lightly crushed
- 1¼ cups water
- 1 tablespoon honey

How to Prepare:

1. In a smaller pan, add juniper berries in 1 cup of water over medium heat and simmer for about 5-10 minutes
2. Strain the tea into a serving mug and stir in honey
3. Serve hot.

Nutritional Values:

Calories 64, Total Fat 0 g, Saturated Fat 0 g, Cholesterol 0 mg, Sodium 1 mg, Total Carbs 17.3 g, Fiber 0 g, Sugar 17.3 g, Protein 0.1 g

Orange Tea

Preparation time: 5 minutes

Total time: 10 minutes

Servings: 1

Ingredients:

- 1 black tea bag
- 1¼ cups boiling water
- 1 mandarin orange, sliced
- ¼ teaspoon ground cinnamon
- 1 tablespoon honey

How to Prepare:

1. Combine all ingredients in a serving mug and steep, covered for 5-10 minutes.
2. Through a mesh strainer, strain the tea and serve.

Nutritional Values:

Calories 67, Total Fat 0 g, Saturated Fat 0 g, Cholesterol 0 mg, Sodium 1 mg, Total Carbs 18.3 g, Fiber 0.6 g, Sugar 17.3 g, Protein 0.1 g

Mint Green Tea

Preparation time: 10 minutes

Total time: 10 minutes

Servings: 2

Ingredients:

- 2½ cups boiling water
- 1 cup fresh mint leaves
- 4 green tea bags
- 2 teaspoons honey

How to Prepare:

1. In a pitcher, add in water, mint and tea bags.
2. Cover and steep for about 5 minutes.
3. Then remove the tea bags from pitcher and pour the tea into two serving mugs
4. Stir in honey and serve hot.

Nutritional Values:

Calories 41, Total Fat 0.3 g, Saturated Fat 0.1 g, Cholesterol 0 mg, Sodium 14 mg, Total Carbs 9.6 g, Fiber 3.1 g, Sugar 5.8 g, Protein 1.5 g

Lemony Ginger Tea

Preparation time: 10 minutes

Cooking time: 15 minutes

Total time: 25 minutes

Servings: 6

Ingredients:

- 8 cups water
- 1 (4-inch) piece fresh ginger, chopped
- 4 lemons, sliced
- 6 cardamom pods, bruised
- 1 cinnamon stick
- 1 whole star anise pod
- 3 tablespoons raw honey

How to Prepare:

1. In a medium-sized saucepan, add in water and bring to a boil over medium-high heat.
2. Add in ginger, lemon slices, and spices and adjust the heat to medium-low.
3. Simmer for about 5-10 minutes.
4. Strain the tea into a pitcher.
5. Stir in honey and serve.

Nutritional Values:

Calories 43, Total Fat 0.2 g, Saturated Fat 0 g, Cholesterol 0 mg, Sodium 1 mg, Total Carbs 11.4 g, Fiber 0.8 g, Sugar 8.9 g, Protein 0.4 g

Lemony Green Tea

Preparation time: 10 minutes

Total time: 10 minutes

Servings: 1

Ingredients:

- 1 (2-inch) lemon zest piece, thinly sliced
- 2 teaspoons boiling water
- 2 teaspoons green tea powder
- ¾ cup hot water
- ½ cup grapefruit juice
- 5 teaspoons lemon juice
- 1 teaspoon honey

How to Prepare:

1. In a large mug, add lemon peel and 2 teaspoons of boiling water and brew, covered for about 3 minutes.
2. Add green tea powder and hot water and stir to combine.
3. Now, add the grapefruit juice, lemon juice, and honey and stir until well blended.
4. Serve hot.

Nutritional Values:

Calories 66, Total Fat 0.3 g, Saturated Fat 0.2 g, Cholesterol 0 mg, Sodium 6 mg, Total Carbs 16.1 g, Fiber 1.5 g, Sugar 14.4 g, Protein 1 g

Ginger & Turmeric Tea

Preparation time: 10 minutes

Total time: 10 minutes

Servings: 2

Ingredients:

- Boiling water, as required
- 4 teaspoons fresh turmeric, grated finely
- 2 teaspoons fresh ginger, grated finely
- ½ cup hot milk
- 2 teaspoons raw honey
- 1 teaspoon vanilla extract
- ¾ teaspoon ground cinnamon

How to Prepare:

1. Fill 2 serving mugs with the boiling water about halfway full.
2. Then divide grated turmeric and ginger into both mugs evenly.
3. Immediately cover the mugs tightly and steep for about 10-15 minutes.
4. Stir in remaining ingredients and serve.

Nutritional Values:

Calories 82, Total Fat 1.8 g, Saturated Fat 0.9 g, Cholesterol 5 mg, Sodium 32 mg, Total Carbs 13.9 g, Fiber 1.6 g, Sugar 9 g, Protein 2.6 g

Passion Fruit Tea

Preparation time: 10 minutes

Cooking time: 10 minutes

Total time: 20 minutes

Servings: 2

Ingredients:

- 2 cups water
- 3 black tea bags
- 4 star anise pods
- 1 cinnamon stick
- 1 cup passionfruit nectar
- 3 tablespoons honey
- 2 tablespoons fresh lemon juice

How to Prepare:

1. In a small-sized saucepan, add in water and bring to a boil.
2. Add tea bags, anise, and cinnamon stick.
3. Now adjust the heat to low and simmer, uncovered for about 5 minutes.
4. Remove tea bags and whole spices.
5. Stir in nectar, honey, and lemon juice and simmer for about 3-5 minutes or until heated completely.
6. Serve hot.

Nutritional Values:

Calories 214, Total Fat 1 g, Saturated Fat 0.2 g, Cholesterol 0 mg, Sodium 44 mg, Total Carbs 53.8 g, Fiber 12.4 g, Sugar 39.4 g, Protein 2.8 g

Spiced Milk Tea

Preparation time: 10 minutes

Cooking time: 25 minutes

Total time: 35 minutes

Servings: 6

Ingredients:

- 1 star anise
- 12 whole cloves
- 7 whole allspices
- 2 cinnamon sticks
- 7 whole white peppercorns
- 1 green cardamom pod, cracked open
- 1 cup water
- 2 tablespoons black tea leaves
- 4 cups milk
- 6-8 teaspoons sugar

How to Prepare:

1. In a pan, add all ingredients except for milk and sugar and bring to a boil.
2. Remove from heat and brew, covered for about 20 minutes.
3. Add in milk and again bring to a boil.
4. Remove from heat and brew, covered for about 5 minutes.
5. Strain the tea into serving mugs and stir in sugar.
6. Serve hot.

Nutritional Values:

Calories 102, Total Fat 3.5 g, Saturated Fat 2 g, Cholesterol 13 mg, Sodium 80 mg, Total Carbs 13.3 g, Fiber 0.7 g, Sugar 11.4 g, Protein 5.4 g

Apple Tea

Preparation time: 10 minutes

Cooking time: 10 minutes

Total time: 20 minutes

Servings: 2

Ingredients:

- 1 cup water
- 1 whole allspice
- 1 cinnamon stick
- honey
- 2 black tea bags
- 1 cup unsweetened apple juice
- 2 tablespoons

How to Prepare:

1. In a small-sized saucepan, add water, allspice, and cinnamon stick and bring to a boil.
2. Add the tea bags, cover, and immediately remove from the heat.
3. Brew for about 2 minutes.
4. Remove allspice, cinnamon stick, and tea bags.
5. Stir in apple juice and honey and cook for about 3-5 minutes or until heated completely.
6. Transfer the tea into mugs and stir in the honey.
7. Serve hot.

Nutritional Values:

Calories 125, Total Fat 0.2 g, Saturated Fat 0 g, Cholesterol 0 mg, Sodium 8 mg, Total Carbs 32.7 g, Fiber 0.8 g, Sugar 30.8 g, Protein 0.2 g

Cranberry Tea

Preparation time: 10 minutes

Cooking time: 25 minutes

Total time: 35 minutes

Servings: 12

Ingredients:

- 4 cups fresh cranberries
- 12 cups water
- 2 whole cinnamon sticks
- 6 whole cloves
- 2 tablespoons fresh lemon juice
- ½ cup fresh orange juice
- ¼ cup honey

How to Prepare:

1. In a large-sized saucepan, add cranberries, water, cinnamon sticks, and cloves over high heat and bring to a boil.

2. Now adjust the heat to low and simmer, covered for about 15-20 minutes.

3. Remove the pan from heat.

4. Strain the tea through a cheesecloth-lined colander.

5. Return the tea into the pan.

6. Add remaining ingredients and stir to combine.

7. Place the pan over medium-low heat and simmer for about 4-5 minutes or until heated completely.

8. Serve hot.

Nutritional Values:

Calories 48, Total Fat 0 g, Saturated Fat 0 g, Cholesterol 0 mg, Sodium 7 mg, Total Carbs 10.6 g, Fiber 1.6 g, Sugar 8.1 g, Protein 0.1 g

HOT ALCOHOLIC COCKTAILS

Hearty soups and delectable bakes can keep you cozy, but hot alcoholic cocktails are sure to warm you up fast. These exciting and enticing recipes combine all the great fall and winter flavors into fun cocktails for you and your friends.

JAMAICA COFFEE COCKTAIL	271
LEMONY WHISKEY	272
SPIKED LATTE	273
BUTTERED RUM	274
SPIKED MATCHA	275
MULLED CIDER	276
MULLED WINE	277
WINE HOT CHOCOLATE	278
BOURBON EGGNOG	280
CRANBERRIES & CINNAMON COCKTAIL	282

Jamaica Coffee Cocktail

Preparation time: 5 minutes

Total time: 5 minutes

Serving: 1

Ingredients:

- 1½ tablespoons coffee-flavored liqueur
- 1½ tablespoons dark rum
- 1 cup hot brewed coffee
- 2 tablespoons whipped cream

How to Prepare:

1. Pour the coffee liqueur and rum into a coffee glass.
2. Fill glass with hot coffee and serve with the topping of whipped cream.

Nutritional Values:

Calories 208, Total Fat 49.4 g, Saturated Fat 5.8 g, Cholesterol 33 mg, Sodium 17 mg, Total Carbs 10.8 g, Fiber 0 g, Sugar 9.9 g, Protein 1 g

Lemony Whiskey

Preparation time: 5 minutes

Cooking time: 5 minutes

Total time: 10 minutes

Servings: 1

Ingredients:

- ¾ cup water
- 2½ tablespoons whiskey
- 2-3 teaspoons honey
- 2-3 teaspoons fresh lemon juice

How to Prepare:

1. In a small-sized saucepan, add water and bring to a simmer.
2. Pour the hot water into a serving mug.
3. In the mug, add the whiskey, honey, and lemon juice and stir until honey is dissolved.
4. Serve immediately.

Nutritional Values:

Calories 151, Total Fat 0.1 g, Saturated Fat 0.1 g, Cholesterol 0 mg, Sodium 3 mg, Total Carbs 11.8 g, Fiber 0.1 g, Sugar 11.8 g, Protein 0.1 g

Spiked Latte

Preparation time: 5 minutes

Cooking time: 5 minutes

Total time: 10 minutes

Servings: 1

Ingredients:

- ½ cup freshly brewed coffee
- 4 tablespoons whole milk
- 4 tablespoons Kahlua
- 1 tablespoons vodka
- 1 tablespoon whipped cream

How to Prepare:

1. In a small-sized saucepan, add in all ingredients except for whipped cream over medium heat and cook until heated, stirring frequently.
2. Pour into a mug and serve hot with the topping of whipped cream.

Nutritional Values:

Calories 319, Total Fat 6.7 g, Saturated Fat 4 g, Cholesterol 22 mg, Sodium 35 mg, Total Carbs 21.3 g, Fiber 0 g, Sugar 21.3 g, Protein 0.4 g

Buttered Rum

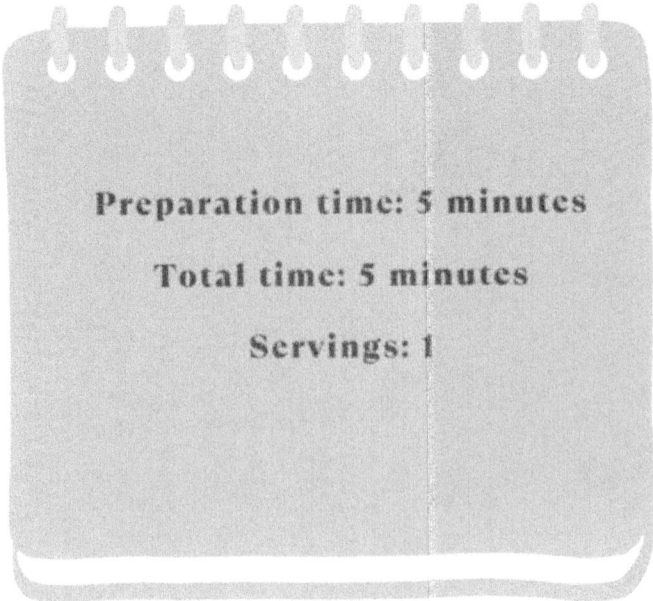

Preparation time: 5 minutes

Total time: 5 minutes

Servings: 1

Ingredients:

- 2 teaspoons packed brown sugar
- 1 tablespoon unsalted butter, softened
- 1 splash pure vanilla extract
- Pinch of ground cinnamon
- Pinch of ground nutmeg
- Pinch of ground allspice
- 4 tablespoons dark rum
- 8 tablespoons hot water
- 1 cinnamon stick

How to Prepare:

1. Place the sugar, butter, vanilla extract, and spices into the bottom of an Irish coffee glass or mug and mix well
2. Pour in the rum and top with hot water.
3. Stir well and serve with the garnishing of cinnamon stick.

Nutritional Values:

Calories 258, Total Fat 11.4 g, Saturated Fat 7.4 g, Cholesterol 31 mg, Sodium 84 mg, Total Carbs 6.2 g, Fiber 0.1 g, Sugar 5.9 g, Protein 0.2 g

Spiked Matcha

Preparation time: 10 minutes

Total time: 10 minutes

Servings: 1

Ingredients:

- 1 teaspoon matcha powder
- ¼ cup hot water
- ¾ cup hot milk
- ½ ounce simple syrup
- 2 tablespoons rum
- 2 tablespoons Rhum

How to Prepare:

1. Through a tea strainer, sift the matcha powder into a serving mug.
2. Slowly add in ¼ cup of boiling water, beating continuously.
3. Add the warm milk, simple syrup, rum, and Rhum and beat until well blended.
4. Serve hot.

Nutritional Values:

Calories 268, Total Fat 3.8 g, Saturated Fat 2.3 g, Cholesterol 16 mg, Sodium 87 mg, Total Carbs 20.9 g, Fiber 0 g, Sugar 8.3 g, Protein 6 g

Mulled Cider

Preparation time: 10 minutes

Cooking time: 1 hour 10 minutes

Total time: 1 hour 20 minutes

Servings: 8

Ingredients:

- 1 whole nutmeg
- 10 allspice berries
- 10 whole cloves
- 2 star anise pods
- 4 cinnamon sticks
- 9-10 cups apple cider
- 1 small orange, cut into slices
- ¼ cup rum

How to Prepare:

1. Heat a large-sized, dry saucepan over medium heat and toast the whole spices for about 2-3 minutes, stirring occasionally.
2. Now adjust the heat to low.
3. In the saucepan, add in the apple cider and orange slices and bring to a low simmer.
4. Simmer for about 1 hour.
5. Divide the rum into serving mugs evenly.
6. Through a fine mesh strainer, strain the cider into mugs and serve.

Nutritional Values:

Calories 162, Total Fat 0.5 g, Saturated Fat 0.1 g, Cholesterol 0 mg, Sodium 10 mg, Total Carbs 36.3 g, Fiber 1.3 g, Sugar 32.6 g, Protein 0.5 g

Mulled Wine

Preparation time: 10 minutes

Cooking time: 3 hours 5 minutes

Total time: 3¼ hours

Servings: 6

Ingredients:

- 1 bottle dry red wine
- ¼ cup brandy
- 1 orange, sliced into rounds
- 2-4 tablespoons sugar
- 8 whole cloves
- 2 cinnamon sticks
- 2 star anise pods

How to Prepare:

1. Add wine, brandy, orange slices, sugar, and spices into a large-sized saucepan and stir to combine.
2. Place the saucepan of wine mixture over medium-high heat and bring to a gentle simmer.
3. Now adjust the heat to low and simmer, covered for up to 3 hours.
4. Through a fine mesh strainer, strain the wine mixture.
5. Serve hot.

Nutritional Values:

Calories 143, Total Fat 0.1 g, Saturated Fat 0 g, Cholesterol 0 mg, Sodium 8 mg, Total Carbs 11.8 g, Fiber 1.1 g, Sugar 8 g, Protein 0.4 g

Wine Hot Chocolate

Preparation time: 10 minutes

Cooking time: 15 minutes

Total time: 25 minutes

Servings: 4

Ingredients:

- 3 cups milk
- 1 cup chocolate chips
- 1 tablespoon dark cocoa powder
- 1 cinnamon stick
- Pinch of salt
- 1½ cups red wine
- 4 tablespoons whipped cream

How to Prepare:

1. In a large-sized pot, add milk, chocolate chips, cocoa powder, salt, and cinnamon stick over medium heat and cook for about 3-5 minutes or until chocolate chips are dissolved completely, stirring continuously.
2. Stir in the wine and immediately adjust the heat to low.
3. Simmer for about 10 minutes, stirring after every 1 minute.
4. Remove the pot of hot chocolate from heat and discard the cinnamon stick.
5. Transfer the hot chocolate into serving mugs.
6. Top with whipped cream and serve.

Nutritional Values:
Calories 436, Total Fat 21 g, Saturated Fat 14 g, Cholesterol 41 mg, Sodium 168 mg, Total Carbs 37.5 g, Fiber 1.8 g, Sugar 30.5 g, Protein 9.8 g

Bourbon Eggnog

Preparation time: 15 minutes

Cooking time: 5 minutes

Total time: 20 minutes

Servings: 2

Ingredients:

- 2 eggs, separated
- ¼ cup granulated sugar
- 2 cups whole milk
- ½ cup heavy cream
- ½ teaspoon pure vanilla extract
- 1 teaspoon nutmeg, grated freshly
- 1/8 teaspoon salt
- ½ cup bourbon

How to Prepare:

1. Add egg yolks in a bowl and with an electric mixer, beat on medium speed until light and smooth.
2. Add in 2 tablespoons of sugar and mix until well blended.
3. Set aside.
4. In a separate bowl, add egg whites and remaining 2 tablespoons of sugar and with an electric mixer, beat until peaks form. Set aside.
5. In a small-sized saucepan, combine milk, cream, vanilla, nutmeg, and salt over medium-low heat and cook until small bubbles start to appear, stirring continuously.
6. Remove from the heat.
7. Slowly pour warm milk mixture into beaten egg yolks and stir until well blended.
8. Add brandy and stir to combine.
9. Fold in whipped egg white mixture and serve.

Nutritional Values:

Calories 544, Total Fat 23.8 g, Saturated Fat 13.1 g, Cholesterol 229 mg, Sodium 319 mg, Total Carbs 37.9 g, Fiber 0.2 g, Sugar 38.6 g, Protein 14.1 g

Cranberries & Cinnamon Cocktail

Preparation time: 10 minutes

Cooking time: 20 minutes

Total time: 30 minutes

Servings: 4

Ingredients:

- 1½ cups cranberry juice cocktail
- 2 cinnamon sticks
- 2 pieces star anise
- ½ cup sugar
- ½ cup fresh cranberries
- 3 cups dry red wine

How to Prepare:

1. In a pan, add cranberry juice cocktail, cinnamon sticks, star anise, and sugar and cook for about 12-15 minutes until sugar is dissolved, stirring frequently.
2. Add cranberries and wine and cook for about 4-5 minutes.
3. Serve hot.

Nutritional Values:

Calories 291, Total Fat 0 g, Saturated Fat 0 g, Cholesterol 0 mg, Sodium 11mg, Total Carbs 42 g, Fiber 0.8 g, Sugar 37.4 g, Protein 0.1 g

HOT NON-ALCOHOLIC COCKTAILS

For those who don't want the alcohol but still want the warmth, these recipes are sure to delight. Creative and tasty concoctions will keep your tastebuds happy, and your hands warm all winter long.

Buttered Pineapple Mocktail 284
Spiced Cider 285
Cranberry Cider 286
Hot Wassail 287
Hot Chocolate 288
Orange Mocha 289
Orange Atole 290
Cranberry Mocktail 291
Gingerbread Latte 292
Raspberry Hot Chocolate 293

Buttered Pineapple Mocktail

Preparation time: 10 minutes

Cooking time: 25 minutes

Total time: 40 minutes

Servings: 6

Ingredients:

- 6 cups pineapple juice
- 2/3 cup orange juice
- 2 tablespoons butter
- 2 teaspoons brown sugar
- 4 cinnamon sticks, broken

How to Prepare:

1. Add in the pineapple juice, orange juice, butter, brown sugar, and cinnamon sticks into a large-sized saucepan and bring to a boil.
2. Now adjust the heat to low and simmer for about 20 minutes.
3. Strain into serving mugs and serve.

Nutritional Values:

Calories 170, Total Fat 4.2 g, Saturated Fat 2.5 g, Cholesterol 10 mg, Sodium 32 mg, Total Carbs 33 g, Fiber 0.5 g, Sugar 25.9 g, Protein 1.1 g

Spiced Cider

Preparation time: 10 minutes

Cooking time: 35 minutes

Total time: 45 minutes

Servings: 4

Ingredients:

- 4 cups apple cider
- 2 star anise pods
- 1 cinnamon stick
- 3 whole cloves
- 3 whole allspices
- 2-3 tablespoons clementine juice

How to Prepare:

1. In a medium-sized saucepan, add all ingredients over medium heat and bring to a boil.
2. Now adjust the heat to low and simmer for about 30 minutes.
3. Strain the spices and serve hot.

Nutritional Values:

Calories 124, Total Fat 0.3 g, Saturated Fat 0.1 g, Cholesterol 0 mg, Sodium 8 mg, Total Carbs 31.3 g, Fiber 1.2 g, Sugar 27.8 g, Protein 0.3 g

Cranberry Cider

Preparation time: 10 minutes

Cooking time: 50 minutes

Total time: 1 hour

Servings: 12

Ingredients:

- 8 cups soft apple cider
- 8 cups unsweetened cranberry juice
- 2 medium oranges, sliced
- 1 (2-inch) piece fresh ginger
- ¼ cup white sugar
- 1 teaspoon whole cloves
- 4 star anise pods
- 3 tablespoon cardamom pods
- 3 cinnamon sticks, broken into pieces

How to Prepare:

1. Add in apple cider and cranberry juice into a large-sized saucepan over medium-high heat and bring to a boil.
2. Add the sugar and spices and stir to combine
3. Now adjust the heat to low and simmer for about 45 minutes.
4. Strain the mixture and serve hot.

Nutritional Values:

Calories 166, Total Fat 0.4 g, Saturated Fat 0.1 g, Cholesterol 0 mg, Sodium 29 mg, Total Carbs 40.9 g, Fiber 1.4 g, Sugar 31.1 g, Protein 0.6 g

Hot Wassail

Preparation time: 15 minutes

Cooking time: 50 minutes

Total time: 1 hour 5 minutes

Servings: 10

Ingredients:

- 2 apples
- 15 whole cloves
- 8 cups apple cider
- 2 cups orange juice
- 1/3 cup lemon juice
- 1 tablespoon light brown sugar
- 4 cinnamon sticks
- ¼ teaspoon ground nutmeg
- ¼ teaspoon ground ginger

How to Prepare:

1. Poke the cloves into the skin of apples on all sides.
2. Place the apples and remaining ingredients over medium-high heat and bring to a boil.
3. Now adjust the heat to medium-low and simmer for about 30-45 minutes.
4. Remove from the heat and discard the apples and whole cloves.
5. Transfer into mugs and serve.

Nutritional Values:

Calories 149, Total Fat 0.8 g, Saturated Fat 0.2 g, Cholesterol 0 mg, Sodium 12 mg, Total Carbs 36.4 g, Fiber 1.9 g, Sugar 31.5 g, Protein 0.7 g

Hot Chocolate

Preparation time: 10 minutes

Cooking time: 10 minutes

Total time: 20 minutes

Servings: 4

Ingredients:

- ¾ cup water
- 3 tablespoons cocoa powder
- 3 cups whole milk
- 6 ounces semisweet chocolate, chopped finely
- 3 tablespoons granulated sugar
- 4 tablespoons whipped cream

How to Prepare:

1. Place water into a medium saucepan over medium-high heat and bring to a boil.
2. Add in cocoa powder and stir vigorously until smooth.
3. Add in milk and again bring to a boil, stirring continuously.
4. Add in chocolate and sugar and cook for about 5 minutes, whisking frequently.
5. Pour the hot chocolate into four serving mugs and serve with the topping of whipped cream.

Nutritional Values:

Calories 400, Total Fat 23.9 g, Saturated Fat 14.2 g, Cholesterol 35 mg, Sodium 85 mg, Total Carbs 46.8 g, Fiber 3.7 g, Sugar 41.9 g, Protein 8.7 g

Orange Mocha

Preparation time: 15 minutes

Cooking time: 5 minutes

Total time: 20 minutes

Servings: 6

Ingredients:

- 3-4 orange peel strips
- 7 whole cloves
- 2 cinnamon sticks
- 2 cups milk
- 2 cups water
- 1/3 cup fresh orange juice
- ½ cup brown sugar
- ¼ cup unsweetened cocoa powder
- 2 tablespoons instant coffee crystals
- ¼ teaspoon vanilla extract

How to Prepare:

1. In a spice bag, wrap the orange peel strips, cinnamon, and cloves.
2. In a large-sized saucepan, add in the spice bag and remaining ingredients except for vanilla extract over medium heat and cook until boiling, stirring continuously.
3. Remove the saucepan of mixture from heat and set aside, covered for about 10 minutes.
4. Discard the spice bag and stir in vanilla extract.
5. Serve hot.

Nutritional Values:

Calories 104, Total Fat 2.3 g, Saturated Fat 1.3 g, Cholesterol 7 mg, Sodium 46 mg, Total Carbs 19.8 g, Fiber 1.5 g, Sugar 16.7 g, Protein 3.5 g

Orange Atole

Preparation time: 10 minutes

Cooking time: 15 minutes

Total time: 25 minutes

Servings: 4

Ingredients:

- 1½ cups water
- 6 tablespoons cornflour, sifted
- 1 cup orange juice, strained
- ½ cup sugar
- 2 cups hot milk

How to Prepare:

1. Blend the water and cornflour in a saucepan until the flour dissolves completely.
2. Place the saucepan over high heat and cook for about 3-5 minutes or until the mixture is thick, stirring continuously.
3. Add the orange juice and sugar and cook for about 2-3 minutes, stirring continuously.
4. Add the milk and stir to combine well.
5. Cook for about 5 minutes, stirring continuously.
6. Serve hot.

Nutritional Values:

Calories 222, Total Fat 3.1 g, Saturated Fat 1.6 g, Cholesterol 10 mg, Sodium 59 mg, Total Carbs 45.8 g, Fiber 0.9 g, Sugar 35.8 g, Protein 5.2 g

Cranberry Mocktail

Preparation time: 10 minutes

Cooking time: 7 minutes

Total time: 17 minutes

Servings: 1

Ingredients:

- ¾ cup cranberry juice
- 1/3 cup orange juice
- 1 (½-inch) piece fresh ginger, peeled
- ½ cinnamon stick
- 2 whole cloves
- 1 teaspoon honey

How to Prepare:

1. Place the cranberry juice, orange juice, ginger, and spices into a small-sized saucepan over medium heat and bring to a gentle simmer.
2. Now adjust the heat to low and simmer for about 2 minutes.
3. Remove the pan of mocktail from heat and stir in the honey.
4. Strain into a serving mug and serve.

Nutritional Values:

Calories 159, Total Fat 0.3 g, Saturated Fat 0.1 g, Cholesterol 0 mg, Sodium 2 mg, Total Carbs 31.4 g, Fiber 6.6 g, Sugar 19.1 g, Protein 0.8 g

Gingerbread Latte

Preparation time: 10 minutes

Total time: 10 minutes

Servings: 2

Ingredients:

- ¾ cup strong-brewed coffee
- 2 tablespoons molasses
- 2 teaspoons sugar
- 1 teaspoon ground cinnamon
- 1 teaspoon ground ginger
- 1½ cups hot milk
- 2 tablespoons whipped cream

How to Prepare:

1. In a glass bowl, combine the coffee, molasses, sugar, and spices and beat until well blended.
2. Divide the coffee mixture into two mugs.
3. Top with milk and serve with the topping of whipped cream.

Nutritional Values:

Calories 215, Total Fat 8.5 g, Saturated Fat 5.2 g, Cholesterol3 2 mg, Sodium 101 mg, Total Carbs 30 g, Fiber 0.7 g, Sugar 23.4 g, Protein 6.6 g

Raspberry Hot Chocolate

Preparation time: 15 minutes

Cooking time: 5 minutes

Total time: 20 minutes

Servings: 4

Ingredients:

- 7 ounces fresh raspberries
- 3 tablespoons icing sugar
- 1 tablespoon water
- 4¼ ounces dark chocolate, chopped finely
- ½ teaspoon vanilla extract
- 3 cups hot whole milk
- 4 tablespoons whipped cream

How to Prepare:

1. Pour water into a small-sized saucepan over medium heat, add raspberries and icing sugar and cook for about 5 minutes, stirring frequently.
2. Through a sieve, strain the raspberry mixture by pressing with the back of a spoon.
3. Discard the seeds.
4. Add in the hot milk, chocolate, and vanilla extract in a blender and let it sit for about 1 minute.
5. Add the cooked raspberries and pulse until frothy.
6. Pour the chocolate mixture into mugs and serve with the topping of whipped cream.

Nutritional Values:

Calories 365, Total Fat 19.9 g, Saturated Fat 12.6 g, Cholesterol 42 mg, Sodium 103 mg, Total Carbs 38.6 g, Fiber 4.2 g, Sugar 33.3 g, Protein 9.1 g

Conclusion

Are you all set to stock up your pantry for winter? Well, our winter dinner recipe collection will definitely help you introduce just the right ingredients into your routine meals and holiday treats. In addition to these winter dinner ideas, you can also try our exclusive holiday recipes from the **Complete Holiday Cookbook**. Winters can be rough and good food can be more comforting than you can imagine. So, eat right and enjoy the best of winter dinners by trying all of our 160 recipes. **You will love them all!**

Made in the USA
Coppell, TX
19 November 2021